8 Press Box
9 A Stand
10 Q Stand
nd Balcony   11 Members' seating

Lord's
My Cricket Home

David Dunbar

with photographs by
Jim Dunbar

My childhood living at Lord's and
personal memories over 60 years

Published by David Dunbar
31 Llanvanor Road, London NW2 2AR UK

020 8455 9612
dgldunbar@aol.com
www.aurelianbooks.com

Requests for permission to reproduce material from this work should be sent to
David Dunbar.

First published 2015
Copyright © 2015 David Dunbar

British Library Cataloguing-in-Publication Data is available.

ISBN 978-0-9933790-0-0

Production and design by **WILD**Guides Ltd., Old Basing, Hampshire UK.
Printed by Dimograf, Poland.

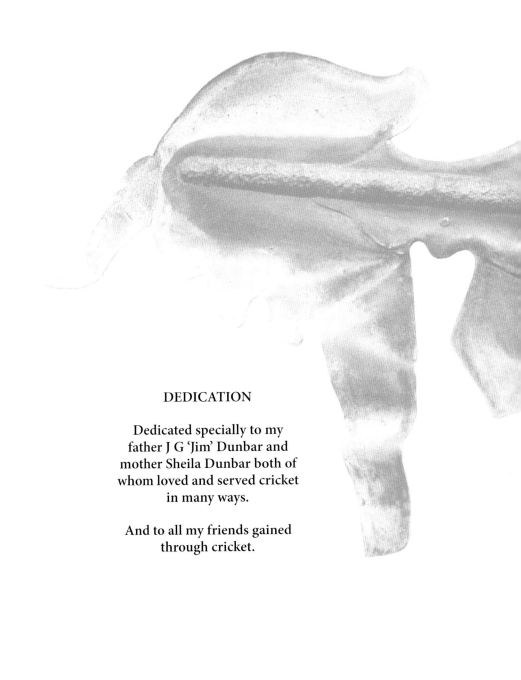

DEDICATION

Dedicated specially to my
father J G 'Jim' Dunbar and
mother Sheila Dunbar both of
whom loved and served cricket
in many ways.

And to all my friends gained
through cricket.

ACKNOWLEDGEMENTS

Most of the photographs in this book were taken by my late father, Jim Dunbar, while he worked as an Assistant Secretary to MCC at Lord's in the 1950s and 1960s. They are a unique record in colour of the happenings around the great cricket ground in the immediate post-war period when life was very different to what it is like nearly seventy years on. Sorting through his large collection of transparencies was an exacting task but essential to remind me of nearly forgotten aspects and incidents of the place, and people who were members of the Lord's 'family'. They were happy days and I am very grateful for this contribution which has greatly enhanced the interest of my book of memories.

Help and advice has come from many people who have given their time and enthusiasm to be involved. Colin Maynard, Deputy Chief Executive of MCC, has given me invaluable guidance and assistance, drawing on his encyclopaedic memory of all things Lord's – the people, events and the buildings. He has also facilitated the marketing and selling of the book. Present Lord's staff including Robert Curphey and Neil Robinson, have generously encouraged me, and provided useful thoughts in seeing this work through to the close of play. Others connected both past and present with Lord's have also guided me, including John and Donald Carr, Stephen Green, Glenys Williams and Veronica Dick. My thanks go to them all and to MCC for kind permission to use some images of pictures from their art collection.

Others who have helped in a numbers of ways include Brian McDowell, Mike Percik, Bridget Clarke, Paul Goldman and Helen Will and Ray Webster at Melbourne CC. Robert Still of WILDGuides Ltd, the designer of this book, has been supremely patient with me amending draft after draft and then producing and publishing a most polished product at the end of the day. To all of them my grateful thanks and appreciation for their kind, friendly and skilful help.

Finally, a huge thank you to my dear wife, Gill, who has had to put up with me monopolising the home computer whilst compiling the book. Alternatively I monopolised the TV when the Sky cricket was on. Infinitely more important was her support whenever I was struggling; I am not a natural or disciplined writer, so her encouragement was critical to getting the job done.

David Dunbar
14 July 2015

INTRODUCTION

Lord's is known as 'The Home of Cricket' and to grow up in a family home which has its own private entrance to Lord's is a truly privileged cricketing upbringing. As a result of his father's appointment as Assistant Secretary of MCC, David Dunbar moved into this special home bordering Lord's, 6 Elm Tree Road, approaching his eighth birthday in the summer of 1951. I believe all who love Lord's Cricket Ground will enjoy David's vivid recollections of Lord's through the 50s and 60s along with the excellent photographs, largely taken by his father Jim. David's love of Lord's has led him to extensively research the history of the Ground and related information and this account should provide new and informative insights for even the keenest Lord's historians.

My own cricket upbringing was equally as privileged and remarkably similar to David's, as I was born in the next door house, 4 Elm Tree Road, in June 1963 soon after my father, Donald Carr, had started as a colleague of Jim Dunbar as an Assistant Secretary at MCC. I too enjoyed private access to the Home of Cricket through the green gates at either end of the cinder pathway that ran between 6 and 8 Elm Tree Road and entered the ground just behind the Warner Stand. I took full advantage of the opportunities presented, watching cricket whenever I could, and enjoying Lord's as a wonderful playground through the off-season. Despite a number of years representing Middlesex, the only ball I ever managed to hit into the Pavilion was a golf ball hit off a door mat whilst practising chipping with my father on the hallowed turf!

Part of my family's good fortune was having the Dunbar family next door as such good friends and neighbours and it resulted in David becoming my godfather and I'm most grateful for his on-going support and friendship.

John Carr
Director, England Cricket Operations
Engand and Wales Cricket Board
June 2015

BATTING ORDER

Coronation Plea from WG
The Old Grand Stand and Printing
Twentieth Century Makeover
The Tavern and the Slope
The Big Green Mound
Lord's Landmark

STUMPS

LORD'S

Thomas Lord 1755–1832

THE TAVERN

1

INTO THE KINGDOM OF LORD'S

OLD SCHOOL

My childhood experiences of Lord's began in April 1949 when my father, J G Dunbar, was appointed an Assistant Secretary of the Marylebone Cricket Club, MCC – for short. A couple of years later my parents came to live at Lord's just before my eighth birthday. The family home for the next twenty-eight years had a private gate in the back garden wall straight into Lord's just behind what was then the A Stand and is now the Warner Stand.

As an only child, this was a cheerful and sunny time of my life although I had little idea how my future was to be influenced by this fortuitous move. In fact, the story spans some sixty years from the early 1950s to the present time and is about Lord's Cricket Ground, the home of cricket in London's St John's Wood. Now, as a member of the club all those years on, the story is still running, with Lord's and cricket featuring in my life and affections. I am grateful to be enjoying this life-long and privileged association.

Father Time wields his inevitable scythe so fleeting memories and reminiscences of a bygone local and social scene are soon lost. The passing

The Lord's Pavilion.

of time rapidly fades our recollections of brief events, and how life and the world used to be. Intended only as a piece of family history I was surprised that several friends, who dipped into an early draft, enthusiastically demanded more and to see a fuller version. So, I have tried to present a very personal and unique view of life in and around Lord's. Rather than repeat well-recorded commentaries and eloquent histories about the game, this is more of a domestic account of random behind-the-scenes happenings, most of which have not, until now, been recorded. Here and there I have indulged in my own thoughts, some mildly indiscreet or irreverent, which are pitched outside the normally perceived box.

Many forests have been felled to make cricket bats and stumps but also for books, newspapers and magazines about the game of cricket, and grand histories about Lord's matches, personalities and treasures still appear with great regularity. Over the years countless great writings and books about Lord's offer almost a lifetime of reading. In writing this book I found useful references in *Pavilions of Splendour, An Architectural History of Lord's* by Duff Hart-Davis published in 2004. There have been three Lord's and this book records the brief lives of the first two grounds in Marylebone and then the third which has occupied the present site for over two hundred years. The development of the ground is meticulously traced and my own recollections dovetail comfortably with the last sixty years covered by this history.

The year 2013 saw two magnificent books hit the shelves. The first was Adam Chadwick's *A Portrait of Lord's* then followed closely by Andrew Strauss's *A Celebration of Lord's*. Primarily picture books, both have plentiful accounts of Lord's past and present and are superbly illustrated records of the public side of the great institution.

Those seeking a formal history of Lord's should defer to Sir Pelham Warner's *Lord's 1787–1945*. *Lord's 1947–1970* by Diana Rait Kerr and Ian Peebles is a comprehensive account, perhaps now real history, covering the main period of my book from the grand perspective of the MCC, Lord's and cricket. For lighter reading *My Lord's*, 1990, edited by Tim Heald offers an eclectic selection of reminiscences and anecdotes by well-known cricketing enthusiasts of the twentieth century. A fascinating little book I discovered only recently is *Recollections of Lord's and the Marylebone Cricket Club* by William H Slatter published in 1914. Slatter was on the Lord's ground staff and writes engagingly about his life and members of his family employed at Lord's in the nineteenth century – wild rabbits on the ground, pony racing at the end of the season, the first mower and the motley characters, from aristocrats to artisans, he encountered in the cricket world.

Lord's is haunted by cricket traditions, history, culture and the spirit of a timeless ever-changing sport. Amongst all the aspects of cricket is limitless material and opportunities for writers, observers and enthusiasts. From earnest analysis and commentary to frivolous and humorous anecdotes, the taste of every reader continues to be indulged. At the mercy of the weather, it is a game of competition, skill, rivalries, excitement, tensions, subtleties, intricacies, unpredictabilities, successes, failures, fun and emotions – not to mention the indecipherable laws! Then, we have the people, with players, spectators, umpires, administrators, the media, and assorted characters, all of whom play or follow the game and create the world of cricket.

The physical heart of MCC was and, of course, still is Lord's Cricket Ground, with its stands and grounds of some seven acres in north London's smart St John's Wood. Lord's is located in the old London Borough of St Marylebone, now part of the City of Westminster. Quite why the St, the sainthood, was not adopted in the club name has yet to be explained to me. In the 1950s MCC was the unrivalled prestigious cricket club and much revered. Moreover, it was the imperial and omnipotent ruling body of world cricket still gripped by the Establishment hand of the old Etonian, token Harrovian and other also-ran public school luminaries allowed in for condescending good measure. At Lord's the warm embers of old Empire still glowed with confidence.

EGG AND TOMATO

Lord's is about pride, so much so that members, even to this day, sport the thick striped 'egg and bacon' ties and blazers with a bizarre lack of embarrassment. (In fact, the bacon red is more of a ripe tomato hue).

The Pavilion retains a unique timeless grandeur and resplendence unmatched by any other sports-

MCC flag.

viewing edifice in the world, perhaps. It is also a humbling monument and example of how the Victorians got things done quickly, having built the Pavilion in a mere seven months and finished in 1890. No planning consents were required and the club went for the cheapest design option.

From this headquarters at Lord's, MCC administered the game, guarded its spirit and decreed the Laws of Cricket throughout the Commonwealth and, indeed, the world. At home England played under the inexplicable red and yellow flag which vaguely imitates the Spanish national flag. No one seems to know how this design came about. In the nineteenth century the club colours and flag were a light blue but then changed, without any recorded explanation, to the present design. In fact it is thought tht the colours may be derived from Nicholson's gin, the proprietor of which, William Nicholson, funded the purchase of the ground. On overseas tours England paraded under the name of MCC and the red cross on a white flag of St George of doomed dragon fame. Coincidentally spectators on their way to the ground pass an imposing statue. The two mythical figures dramatically pose on the roundabout opposite St John's Wood church.

MCC perpetuated, and still do, a formal atmosphere, exemplified by its curt and authoritarian communications both with members and the public.

'Keep off the grass. Do not move when bowling at this end. Wear a jacket. Wear a tie. Wear a shirt. No ripped jeans' (nothing about actually wearing trousers) 'No trumpet playing' and so on and so on. I find it perverse that wearing the hideous broad striped egg and tomato tie, let alone the garish blazer is not banned. Every forbidden thing was, and mostly still is 'By order of the Secretary' (or the Chief Executive now) or, for indictable offences, 'By order of the Committee'. More recently 'Mobile devices may be confiscated' (and crushed under the heavy roller – my words) as will be an excess of the alcohol allowance in your picnic basket. Get caught lending your membership pass to a pal and you'll probably meet the same fate as your mobile (and quite right too).

The MCC Rule book is sent regularly to members – lest we forget. No private club can equal the dazzling and intricate array of misdemeanours for which members may be subjected to 'disciplinary action'. I wager it is the most unread mass publication on the planet, but six of the best for transgressors. Recently the Long Room tables were strewn with extravagant glossy leaflets intricately explaining what dress attire was and was not permitted in the Pavilion – separate sections for each gender, and well illustrated to leave no doubt. Just at that moment a lady passes me wearing grubby flip flops decorated with little pink plastic flowers. Long live the Revolution!

Design based on the
'Keep Britain Tidy' campaign.

On another occasion I was charmingly ticked off by a steward for standing on a yellow line on the steps outside the Committee Room while watching cricket in a near empty ground. 'Have stood here for the last forty five years, on and off', I explained.

'Health and Safety, sir', the steward, very politely but resolutely replied. 'Bollocks', I retorted courageously. 'I quite agree, sir, but please take a seat'. They have even allowed a Health & Safety memorial plaque to scar the back wall of the Pavilion. Just behind the intimidation it is a user-friendly place, although it is amazing the waiting list for membership is always so long!

Keep off the grass – more Rules!

None of this is new. Post-war ground entrance control tended towards the over-zealous and often downright officious. No one was immune. Long ago Prince Philip, was once impeded by a steward from entering Lord's because he failed to produce his membership pass. 'Prince Philip. Oh, yes, sir', intoned the implacable gateman. 'And I am the man in the moon', or words to that effect, so the story goes. HRH did eventually get in!

THE SELECTION

Despite the post-war gloom, cricket was still extraordinarily popular and rapidly reviving, with Lord's a central attraction. The MCC recognised the need to reinforce its administration and bring new life to its stands and buildings with immediate coats of paint and eventual redevelopment. Hence the expansion of the administrative team and creation of new posts.

Dad's recruitment process seems to have been surprisingly enlightened for its time. Along with several other short-listed candidates, he spent a day being interviewed and 'observed' by the powers-that-were. In fact, the real power was wielded by the then Secretary, Colonel R S (Rowan Scope – names I never heard used, not even by his wife) Rait Kerr. He ruled the roost with unabashed military efficiency and authority. Behind a somewhat austere façade and an abrupt military bearing was a man of incisive thinking, considerable ability

Colonel R S Rait Kerr in The Committee Room (by John Ward)

and, also, kindness. On his return home from his day at Lord's Dad had been encouraged that at lunchtime orders were issued that he should sit next to the Colonel. They had got on well so the candidate was cautiously optimistic.

His credentials certainly stood out as he had qualified as a chartered surveyor in 1938 and, having risen to the rank of wartime major in the Sappers, was considered by the Colonel to be ideal for the job. Incidentally the Colonel had also been a Royal Engineer in his military days. It probably helped also that Dad was a keen sportsman playing club cricket or football every weekend. Very shortly his appointment was confirmed and without a moment's hesitation he relinquished his civil service job with the Ministry of Works at Lambeth to head north of the river. His wide circle of sporting friends turned instantly green in the belief he had landed the enviably perfect dream job – working at Lord's; so he also believed.

Jim Dunbar in 1953.

2

HOME BY LORD'S

HAUNTED AT GROVE END

In the summer of 1949 we were living in Putney. My father began commuting on the 74 bus, which trundled from the bridge where the boat race starts to the roundabout by Lord's, for a fare of seven old pennies, a maroon coloured ticket and a good hour's journey. Park Lane, en route, was still a single two-way street to the east of Hyde Park. Baker Street remained two-way for many more years and the erstwhile Marks and Spencer's headquarters building, half way down, was a huge bomb-site scar in the ground. Even so it was a relatively quick trip compared with modern-day London travel.

Our family social life at weekends revolved around sport. In the winter months we watched Old Carthusian soccer battles for the Arthur Dunn Cup and also the Corinthian Casuals who played at the Oval. On summer Sundays father bowled for nomadic cricket teams – the Butterflies CC, I Zingari and Grasshoppers wandering the south of England. 'Jim', as he was universally

David Dunbar and father Jim Dunbar – the best photograph taken by my mother in 1953.

known by all his friends and acquaintances had scored goals for the OCs and bowled medium-quick seamers. Out-swingers and in-swingers were his specialty and there was no mystique about 'reverse swing' as far as he was concerned. Based on the philosophy of consistently aiming at the off-stump his hauls of wickets were phenomenal. Before the War he had a county trial with Sussex but his father thought he ought to concentrate on work so his playing talents were never fully exploited.

Both the Lord's administration and he were keen for us to move closer to the job – live over the shop, so to speak. The first idea was that an old house, MCC owned, at 12 Grove End Road should be renovated. At that time MCC's family silver, now virtually all sold, consisted of all the adjoining properties from the corner with St John's Wood Road to Elm Tree Road and along the south side of the latter. With the benefit of hindsight many of MCC's more recent development plans and aspirations might have had a greater chance of fruition had they retained these properties. Instead they were sold off piecemeal over a period of many years to raise easy funding for modernisation projects. All sorts of ideas for redevelopment behind the Pavilion have fallen by the wayside. There is space for an extension of the administrative offices, a leisure centre, another Real Tennis court, an underground car park and more.

Number twelve was an early nineteenth century regency 'white elephant' as my father described it. It was my first memory of Lord's. My mother and I were taken to have a look at the huge house which had been unoccupied for over ten years. Through a gate in the wall a jungle greeted us. I remember steps up to an imposing front door with a brass knocker formed by two naked cherubs dangling from the mouth of a bearded sun god.

We entered into a cavernous hallway of dark wood panelling and marbled floor and pillars. The main reception room, once magnificent, was equally gloomy with much timber and a minstrel's gallery and piles of broken mirror glass littering the creaking and rotten floorboards. Upstairs was hazardous with missing floors, debris from collapsed ceilings, rotting windows and carpets of pigeon droppings. All it lacked was Miss Havisham sulking in a corner clad in her yellowing wedding dress. Only the bathroom was amazingly intact with vast mirrors set in black and white marbled columns and a bath practically big enough for an entire cricket team to cosy up in. Once upon a time it had been

The brass door knocker from 12 Grove End Road.

a magnificent home made over in a lavish style possibly by a banker who made money in Brazil. It was, however, oppressively creepy with the atmosphere of a seemingly uneasy past. The roof of the house was crowned with a circular balcony surrounding a cupola topped by a weather vane.

The extensive back garden, neglected for many years, was an impenetrable wilderness of trees, brambles and vestiges of grand design landscaping of a bygone era. In the centre of what was once a lawn, a circle of York stones surrounded a beautiful and perhaps once loved willow tree weeping to the ground. Now part of the Coronation Garden sixty years later, it still cries.

I was seven when I first saw the house and for many years after I had vivid nightmares about being trapped inside. What no one had told us, until some years later, was that number twelve was supposed to be haunted – something to do with the weather vane. The supernatural has never been high on my terror list but that house was not good. And when it was finally demolished, none of the Lord's works staff would go anywhere near it. As a film set, Hitchcock would have relished it and, nowadays, Grade One protection would be imposed without hesitation. According to records it was built in 1823 by the Eyre family Estate which owned a large part of St John's Wood, including the fields which became the cricket ground. Lord's rumours abounded that there were tunnels linking the grand Regency houses along Grove End Road. St John's Wood had a reputation for fun, frolics and illicit liaisons in Victorian times so probably some intriguing history lies buried. Occasionally the existence of a tunnel under the main ground at Lord's was alluded to but such flights of folklore

Lord's circa 1829. To the right of the first pavilion is the 'haunted' house at 12 Grove End Road and to the far right the original house on the site of our home at 6 Elm Tree Road.

and fantasy are unproven and no unexplained subsidence has ever appeared on the ground – as yet.

OUR LOCATION, LOCATION

Much to my parents' relief with 'slipping foundations' the house of horrors was condemned as structurally unsound, so MCC had a rethink. Just round the corner a wartime incendiary bomb had gutted the old house at number 6 Elm Tree Road in 1945. MCC decided to demolish it and build us a brand new home.

Tight post-war building restrictions and shortages of materials did not impede progress – only two storeys and only one lavatory were permitted.

The old A Stand now replaced by the Warner Stand.

View from my bedroom window towards Lord's with the Warner Stand, Pavilion and Memorial Gallery in the background. The steps in the right foreground lead up to a Victorian viewing platform originally with a tiled roof.

18

In the early 19th century the Lord's ground had a bad reputation for a very bumpy surface. Sheep mowed the grass somewhat inefficiently.

So Dad just designed gaps here and there for stairs to an attic and had them put in some years later. In spite of these controls it was very well built, with massive roof and floor timbers which by latter day standards would stretch to several houses. I remember the site foreman saying, 'That roof will last a thousand years'. How exciting to watch the foundations being dug and then your home gradually rising from the ground – just for us. About ten months later the house was constructed and ready for us in the summer of 1951. The brass door knocker, which could awaken the dead, eventually found its way from number 12 to number 6 and many years later was rescued from squatters and now hangs on the front door of a Dorset country cottage.

From our upstairs bedrooms the Lord's view was over the old single tier A Stand towards the Tavern scoreboard but only in the winter when the trees were leafless. Those trees, surrounding the walled back garden, created a tranquil rural illusion very close to the centre of London but, much more importantly, in the shadow of Lord's. Talking of tunnels, at the end of our garden, which also backed onto number 12, there was a strange derelict conservatory with steps down to a murky basement, possibly an ice cellar, and a walled-up entrance which led to, who knew where? I was forbidden to explore the unsafe building. Soon the works staff were commandeered to pour tons of concrete down the hole so the mystery was sealed away forever.

CRICKET, LOVELY CRICKET

At the side of our house was a wide unsurfaced driveway between numbers 6 and 8 Elm Tree Road leading into Lord's. I have a nostalgic fantasy that perhaps this was the track along which sheep were driven by Thomas Lord to 'mow' his ground before a match. An old farm cottage and outbuildings remain to this day just opposite number 6. Perhaps each evening the farmer gathered up his sheep from the ground and ducks from the ponds on the Nursery Ground area and locked them away safe from marauding foxes.

At each end of the drive were high double wooden gates painted green, both with small wicket gates. The Lord's statutory grass green paint was used on all the ground gates and everywhere else except the spectator benches. The hue was similar to the green on the old Southern Region railway carriages. It was perhaps a little bland but it gave the illusion of a rural village green setting. The drive was prescribed as an emergency exit for Lord's but never used by the public and came to have other purposes. There was a line of mature pear trees which produced consistently inedible fruit. Dad went to work through a gate in our back garden wall into the drive and then into Lord's just behind where the Warner Stand was built. We had a private, almost secret, entrance to Lord's at all times.

A large wooden shed which once housed mowers somewhere on the far side of Lord's was dismantled and reassembled in the drive to become our garage. There was plenty of space to park the family caravan. The Lord's gardeners, Messrs Stanhope and Spalding, dumped their horticultural waste on a series of compost heaps along one side.

But, most crucially, here was fifty yards of level waste land. Father announced this was to be the real and best wicket of Lord's. We were to create an artificial surface for a cricket practice net. Although this was on MCC land no permission was sought as, although everyone knew, in those days a good idea was never suppressed. During our first winter living there large barrow loads of clinker and ash were transported from the boiler house under the Pavilion extension.

Rain stops play on the main ground. Often several inches of water remained, flooding the ground in front of The Tavern. Water often spilled under the protective covers. The sight screens were painted a pale 'duck egg' green for a while.

Only eight years old, I laboured hard for many hours sieving and mixing the fine ash with a binding loam. A twenty-two yard strip was dug out and levelled. The heavy motorised roller trundled from the Nursery End to compact the mixture for ten yards of coconut matting to be pegged over the surface. Spare netting and posts were requisitioned with the help of the head groundsman.

Cricket is meant to be about sunshine but rain has swept down most of this mid-summer morning. It is Test Match time at Lord's, or it should be. Spectators shiver beneath their brollies which drip water down the necks of their soggy neighbours. Others shelter under the gloomy stands while their seats get too soaked to sit on. The covers out on the middle collect puddles which seep through to the wicket – the outfield squelches, and is almost flooded in front of the Tavern. The helpless ground staff huddle in disconsolate groups. The heavy grey skies brighten just a little but not much; the almost invisible drizzle is easing. At least the ground isn't a total white-out as in a previous July when a hail storm obliterated the grass like an Alpine winter. 'Cricket, lovely cricket' – as Lord Beginner's calypso song goes.

The players in the dry warm Pavilion take 'an early lunch' but time passes slowly. The muffled voice, and largely unintelligible, public address system announces the umpires will inspect the wicket at 3 o'clock. (In the 1950s and 1960s the Decca acoustic boffins attempted many state-of-the art innovations to the loudspeakers in order to combat the inaudible echoes which resonated around the stands but only with very limited success!) Everywhere is wet, unplayable, so, not much cricket at Lord's today.

But, what is this noise that can be heard from just behind the old low A Stand? Surely not the unmistakeable sound of leather against willow,

From the mid-1960s the ground was regularly dug to install better drainage systems. The herring-bone patterns left an almost permanent scar on the ground which gradually improved the effects of heavy soaking rain.

ball against bat, and endless appeals reverberating distantly in the ears of the frustrated crowd. Hidden behind some high green gates of the unused exit from the ground are three small boys cheerfully playing their own much more exciting 'Test Match'. Their wicket and net are all-weather, not spoiled by the miserably inclement conditions and the cricket goes on all day. We have no time to worry about what happens just the length of a couple of pitches away – it is more fun to play than watch the rain.

For a good ten years this was the Lord's wicket – true, quite quick, but taking spin and so well drained play was never stopped. A wicket you have prepared yourself is always the best. Here was the centre of my exciting cricketing world.

Friend Nick Samuelson tries out the real Lord's (artificial) pitch. The gate behind was our private access to Lord's – the Pavilion in the background

With my best school friends John Kearsey, Tom Lowenstein and others we spent all daylight hours practising here. Real time fantasy games of net cricket often led to brief suspensions of friendship. At the end of a long afternoon in the net the call was – 'Last over, last man in, eight runs to win, all the fielders on the boundary'. The run scoring, if any, off each shot had to be agreed. Lbws and catches were never conclusively decided. And what about run-outs?

Tom Lowenstein, Mike Griffith (subsequent MCC President) and David Dunbar ready for the nets.

The castling of the middle stump was about the only winning certainty unless, of course, it was a no-ball! By close of play we were exhausted and grimy with dust and grit from the bowling end, which did not have the comfort of matting.

WARNER AND MAY

The net did not go unnoticed and the great Surrey and England batsman, Peter May, faced my deadly bowling on more than one occasion with, of course, nonchalant ease. Peter was more than partial to such a predictable batting wicket and always advised me to follow his mantra of 'When in doubt, push out!' Sir Pelham Warner, the first cricketer to be knighted, could never resist a go in the net as his grandson, Michael, often came for an afternoon in preference to watching the cricket over the wall. Michael bowled the last ball ever received by his grandfather, aged 82, who played it straight off the middle. I don't think he even took off his hat. Formality reigned supreme in those days and I was expected to call him and, indeed, most adults 'sir' which eventually became second nature. It was a deferential world based on position and class but I never quite deduced on which side of the Lord's wall our family belonged. In reality we lived on both sides and my father managed to be popular with the senior hierarchy of Committee but was equally accepted by those who worked for him.

We were blessed with commendably tolerant next-door neighbours, Mr and Mrs Hilton, both eminent consultant doctors. Apparently he spoke seven European languages fluently and others quite well. Without complaint, they

'Plum' Warner   Peter May

The Ben Warsop Bat Factory in St John's Wood

ANTI-CLOCKWISE FROM LEFT: *Willow plantation; seasoning the raw timber; splitting into bat lengths; shaping the blade; handles attached and bound with twine.*

BOTTOM: *The finished bat.*

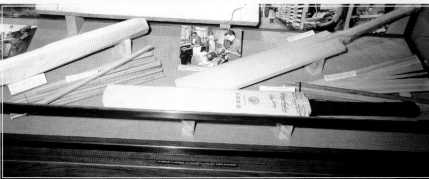

gallantly survived the occasional rogue cricket ball, which evaded the netting only to fly over their garden wall and bounce across the lawn amongst the deck chairs. Luckily, I missed their corgies which menacingly roamed their garden refusing to give back our ball – yappy dogs bred to herd cows in Wales, but with no sense of humour.

BATS AND BALLS

My first cricket bat, a size four which still lives in the attic, came from the Ben Warsop factory in Grove Gardens just off Park Road, only a few hundred yards from Lord's. Its location was behind a block of flats on part of the second Lord's site after it moved from Dorset Square in 1811, being displaced by the new Regent's canal three years later. The bat lasted several years thanks to periodic visits to the bat hospital in the Pavilion. Cracks were glued up and the blade bound with twine and a special material resembling old vellum.

Warsops, founded in 1870, had a high reputation as they supplied Harrods, Lord's and public schools, and their bats were used in Test Matches. As far I can recollect the raw willow trunks were sawn up and stored on the ground floor to season, and upstairs the bats were manufactured. Seeing them made by hand one appreciated the skill of the craftsmen and the value of a treasured bat and the runs that it was going to score. The company did not succumb to competition from the larger manufacturers, eventually moving to a new home near Chelmsford in the early 1960s. Now their bespoke handmade bats are much sought after and, along with the sale of other cricket equipment, enable the business to flourish. Their old factory was occupied by a building company, Kinnimont Ltd, until its demolition in 2010 to make way for luxury flats.

The remains of my first cricket bat made by Warsops.

Len Muncer, Glamorgan CCC, coached at Lord's and ran a cricket equipment shop in St John's Wood.

Real leather cricket balls got scuffed up too quickly on our matting and cinders so we used an artificial ball made by Chingford. Coming in kids' size of 4¾ ounces and full size it was manufactured in some sort of viciously hard indestructible plastic which never lost its shape. The only drawback was that the white nylon-type 'seam' wore away completely after a few hours play. Chingford moved to making hockey balls of worldwide repute.

Len Muncer, the Glamorgan county cricketer, ran a sports equipment business from a cramped half frontage shop, now a hairdresser's, in the parade under Strathmore Court opposite St John's Wood church and the roundabout. Lord's had no shop outlet so, for at least twenty years, all my cricketing gear came from Len's place. If you couldn't see what you wanted he would disappear into the back storeroom always to emerge with the exact item. Vivid is the memory of visiting the shop to buy my first jockstrap and box – as a young teenager, the embarrassment was excruciating!

EASTER COACHING

For me, one special highlight of the Lord's year was the Easter holiday coaching classes for members' sons and friends. It was boys only from the ages of 8 to 18 – with not a female in sight; although my mother always reminded us she played lots of cricket at school! The three day courses in the 1950s were made up of half hour sessions for bowling, batting and fielding, repeated in the afternoon with lectures on captaincy, cricket history and some other topics so riveting I can't remember.

Padding up: David Dunbar, Richard Best and Mark Godson.

The 'Maniacs' ground at Charterhouse School.
Maniacs were the school's third and fourth elevens
which played here or away against local Surrey
villages. Built on a sandstone plateau wickets were
fast, true and very quick drying.

Sheila Dunbar and David in 1960 at Charterhouse.

Wet weather could be a problem as nearly all
the nets were open air on the Nursery End car
park – coconut matting on rolled gravel and
cinders. Rain soaked through instantly. If it
really rained there were some covered nets with
matting wickets under the Mound Stand, in the
old arbours by the Grace Gate and elsewhere
scattered around the ground. MCC employed
an impressive array of former county and test
professionals. Bill Voce and Doug Wright stand
out in my memory along with current Middlesex
and other county players. The head coach for
many years was a former Middlesex player, Bill
Watkins, affectionately known as Watty, who led
by example with genial authority, enthusiasm and
patience. I had a number of friends from the Hall
School at Swiss Cottage and then Charterhouse
to stay for the courses. They were intense and
exhausting, but great fun, and helped to start the
season trying to play the right way.

Such was my enthusiasm that I attempted to
sustain form in the winter months by going to
the Alexandra Palace indoor cricket school. It

Doug Wright succeeded
George Geary as
Charterhouse cricket coach
in 1959. Doug played for Kent
and England from 1938–47
as an almost unplayable fast
legspin bowler.

Easter Classes in the 1950s

MAIN PICTURE: *Batting nets, coconut matting on rolled boiler room clinker, on the Nursery Ground car park. In wet weather covered nets were installed under the arbours in the background and also in the Tea Gardens by the Grace Gates.*

LEFT, TOP TO BOTTOM: *Head coach Bill 'Watty' Watkins, imparts his cricket wisdom during a group session; The Indoor Cricket Schools built in 1977; A young hopeful under the watchful eye of Ted Whitfield, former Surrey CCC player.*

An ancient bowling machine, probably invented during the Roman occupation.

Fielding practice with the 'cradle'.

David Dunbar practices his leg breaks.

was next to the old TV studios. I can remember trudging grimly through the snow up to Muswell Hill to reach the then almost derelict shell of the Palace. The indoor nets were good enough and several well-known players passed their off-season time there including Fred Titmus, the Middlesex and England spinner, who told me if I 'bowled like that I would be hit everywhere'.

My father was a skilful draughtsman and he copied this 19th century monograph for a History of the Butterflies Cricket Club.

Ultimately, my cricketing career had few notable achievements. I did manage a haul of nine wickets for the Charterhouse Under 15 team against Guildford Grammar School. All my cricket master, 'Creeps' Crawford, said afterwards was, 'Good thing their umpire didn't know the lbw law properly'. The Grammar School has the distinction of recording the first written documentary evidence relating to cricket dating back to 1550.

I started the 1961 season in the Charterhouse School 1st eleven as a leg break bowler – this was achieved on the strength of bowling Richard Gilliat for a second-ball duck in a school trial. Richard was poised for a distinguished cricketing career with Oxford University followed by over 250 games for Hampshire. In contrast, although I took several wickets in three matches, at least eight catches were dropped off my bowling. I was sacrificed to languish in the 2nds for the rest of the season. Meanwhile, a useless bunch of fielders stayed in the side safe in the knowledge that half the team was unlikely to be demoted for dropping catches. A hard but possibly necessary lesson for life later on.

For several years after leaving school I played occasionally for the Butterflies CC and Grasshoppers CC, both nomadic clubs with no home but quite grand credentials. The former necessitated an education at one of six public schools (Eton, Harrow, Charterhouse, Winchester, Westminster or Rugby) and the Grasshoppers needed a Surrey connection. The Butterflies played the Eton Ramblers at the Hurlingham Club to celebrate their joint centenaries in 1962. A few overs before lunch my father, who was captaining, put me on to bowl. Much to his surprise, and mine, I took several very quick wickets. The opposition was infuriated, not it seems with their failing batters but, for some weird inexplicable reason, with me! During the interval Dad was surreptitiously approached by a member of the aggrieved team saying that he had been delegated by his captain to suggest that, '… It might make a better game of it if someone else bowled after lunch'. They should have known better. We took the field again in a state of suppressed amusement but, regrettably, a slap-up Hurlingham lunch rendered me incapable of furthering my success although we finally won the match comfortably. Little did I think that, fifty years on, I would be dining in the Long Room to celebrate the Butterflies' 150th Anniversary. According to records assembled by my father, 39 Butterflies have played for England, mostly in the nineteenth century.

STRAWBERRIES, A CAT AND TWO TORTOISES

Back home, one nice perk of the job was that every summer George Newman, a committee member, brought the three Secretaries crates of punnets full of fresh strawberries from his farm – a much anticipated treat. Grown on straw they had that sharp sweet taste so typical of the real English fruit. It is hard to remember that the strawberry season in those days lasted a brief few weeks. Of course, the year-round supermarket availability now means we have the tasteless, mushy, imported versions whenever we want. George also had a farm cat called Sammy who had tendencies towards farmer George's prize ducklings and was heading for a terminal ducking in their pond. My father heard about the problem and offered to adopt this huge long-haired black cat. He was a lovely creature, docile and fearless, who lived a double life partly with us but also in the Pavilion boiler room where staff fed him, he kept warm and made himself useful by catching the occasional mouse. In the twenty-first century I imagine a Pavilion cat is an unlikely management tool for controlling basement rodents.

A few months after his arrival, Sammy disappeared, failing to return home one morning. I was distraught – what misery and despair. All Lord's was put on alert and everyone searched. Nothing. But, ten days later he was discovered trapped in the emergency water supply 'tank' at the back of the squash courts. This was built during the war for the fire brigades to take extra fire-fighting water during the blitz. Like a 30 yard open-air swimming pool sloping down to one end, it was sunk into the ground but surrounded by a six foot brick wall. Fortunately, there was water stagnating only at the deep end. Our idiot pet had probably gone for a pigeon or more likely a kitten-hood memory rekindled by the sight of a stray mallard from Regent's Park and could not escape. He was emaciated but cheerful. As a result the tank was filled in to enlarge the West Gate, now number 6, car park. Some buttresses of the walls still remain as part of the boundary with the adjoining house.

Sammy enjoyed watching cricket. From time to time he strolled on to the ground during a match. He also made a nonchalant appearance on a sunny Saturday afternoon during an Australian Test Match when he wandered out to the middle in front of some thirty thousand spectators. Umpires' and players' efforts to shoo him off took time. 'Cat ch'it', took on a new meaning! He knew every nook and cranny of the ground so evaded capture and eventually sidled off between the old Press Box and A Stand to considerable applause. I recently found an obituary in Wisden about a Lord's cat called Peter, who exactly matched Sammy's description. So perhaps the record needs to be straightened after all these years or was it a stray from the Tavern attempting a grab at the limelight?

Our garden at number 6 Elm Tree Road where tortoises roamed free.

Lola, the Lord's car park foundling tortoise, and Harrods Tommy on the right.

When we moved from our Putney flat to a home with a garden I was promised a tortoise. Being completely walled, our garden was inescapably tortoise-proof so off we went to, of all places, Harrods, which had a magical and thriving pet department on the fourth floor. It was like a miniature zoo stocked with furry creatures, exotic birds and colourful tropical fish and where, I discovered some many years later, you could even buy lion cubs. Now it has just a science dog food and cat litter section. We returned with a very good quality, quite large, tortoise who was unimaginatively named Tommy. He cheerfully settled in our garden where he gorged himself on dandelion leaves, salads, chopped apple and my mother's seedlings.

Some years later during a Test match a tortoise was discovered wandering under parked cars behind the Pavilion. How the unlikely intruder got there will forever remain a mystery. The Lord's Lost Property Office, being more familiar with ownerless umbrellas than livestock, but being well-informed, concluded young Dunbar's Tommy must have escaped and duly delivered the creature to our garden – to join Tommy. The mysterious Lola, as she was named, and I forget why or was it connected with my father's admiration for a certain famous film star, was never claimed so she was adopted by us. Regrettably, Wisden never acknowledged Lola the Lord's tortoise. One day, several years later, my mother heard a clunking noise in the garden and on investigation found Lola balancing nearly on top. They had been together quite a while so there had been a question mark over their genders. Sexing a tortoise can be tricky, except perhaps to other tortoises. The only tinge of sadness was the non-appearance of any eggs. They both lived with us happily ever after; well, for at least twenty years until my parents left Elm Tree Road and the tortoises were pensioned off to a friend's smart garden in Highgate.

NEIGHBOURS

MCC built another house next door to us at number 4 Elm Tree Road which was occupied by successive Assistant Secretaries and their families. First came Billy Griffith and family; son Mike was a contemporary and went on to a stylish and distinguished cricket career, eventually becoming President of MCC in 2012. Subsequently, they moved to number 20, which was the designated accommodation when Billy was appointed Secretary on the retirement of Ronnie Aird in 1962. Shadowed by the back of the Grand Stand, it had a somewhat sombre aspect, not helped by the green painted windows. Previously, the Secretaries were allotted a grander early 19th century house next-door at number 22. MCC raised money by selling this property which, with its large garden, had space for three 'little boxes' – modern houses which were eventually gentrified by the addition of euro-style window shutters and are now worth millions. My father had aspired to the senior job at Lord's but the emphasis began moving towards a preference for Secretaries with first class cricket experience. He was very disappointed to say the least.

Ronnie Aird, MCC Secretary from 1952 to 1962, takes a few minutes off work to demonstrate his bowling skills. Ted Swannell, head groundsman, dutifully admires from a safe distance.

Donald Carr, recently a Derbyshire and England cricketer, succeeded Billy and so he and his wife Stella moved in next door. His England team's earlier exploits in Pakistan did not seem to impede his appointment a few years later. During a Test Match against Pakistan the appalling umpiring decisions against his side had provoked an audacious team protest. An evening operation was masterminded to install a strategically placed bucket of water over the door of said umpire's hotel bedroom door. There were other press versions but Donald assures me this is the correct one. A huge international incident ensued but justice was served, even if it was not so good on his CV for Lord's.

Soon after the Carrs' arrival at Lord's, along came baby John, brother to Diana, and I was invited to be a godparent. Although I had absolutely no influence over his cricketing career I am proud to say John was an entertaining batsman. Oxford and Middlesex were not a problem, although with some dubious coaching, he developed possibly the most unusually original, some might say bizarre, batting stance known to the game. He subbed in a Benson and Hedges final at Lord's on one occasion and took an agile catch right in front of the Pavilion with a full house of members. Gubby Allen generously remarked afterwards that he had 'made it look too easy'. In 1994 at the end of a freak season of 27 innings for Middlesex with ten not-outs John averaged 90, just a whisker ahead of Brian Lara and the framed newspaper cutting of the end of season averages hang proudly at his home – in the loo, of course, where all modest people commemorate their greatest successes.

Donald Carr descends from the Pavilion steps to take the Lord's field.

Young John Carr with father Donald.

3

JOB OF A LIFETIME

THE DUTIES (or death by committees)

By modern day standards, and especially to those familiar with twenty-first century cricket administration, Father's duties were staggeringly extensive but haphazardly allocated. His position as Assistant Secretary was, in effect, jointly second in command with Ronnie Aird. The first ritual of the day was opening the post by the Secretary, Colonel Rait Kerr, and his two Assistants in the Committee Room. This meant that all three had a very clear idea of what was going on in the entire organisation, namely, who was doing what, or not, as was more often the case. The management was close, personal and well-informed, and continued in this mode through the Secretariat of Aird and Griffith for many years.

People often asked my father what he did in the winter when there was no cricket. His rueful answer was always one word – 'committees'. In fact, much of his life was consumed by attending MCC committee and sub-committee meetings. Reporting, minuting, servicing and listening to the droning meant

In the Committee Room (l to r) Gubby Allen, Sir Alec Douglas Home and Secretary, Billy Griffith.

Winter at the 'free' seats – the old power station chimney in the background.

A bleak winter's day at Lord's. Jim Dunbar's photograph has been used on postcards and Lord's Christmas cards more than once.

Jim Dunbar in the MCC Committee Room.

The Committee hard at work watching a match.

that he often came home long after normal office hours. For example, the Laws of Cricket were regularly discussed. He often wondered why there had to be so much talk about the lbw rule – as a bowler, he believed in the batsman walking if the umpire thought the ball would have hit the stumps. Did it really matter where the wretched thing bounced, if at all? What could be simpler, other than Hawkeye! With modern day batting techniques of padding up against a ball certainly about to hit the stumps, a five day test match would probably not last a day.

MCC had always boasted committee members of impeccable pedigree and standing. Silver spoons clattered everywhere. Usually with impeccable ancestry, unrivalled connections and expertise, most were successful top men, smooth and very charming. Most were even clever, but a few were a hindrance because they treated Lord's as a hobby or had little understanding of real life and how to run an organisation. Nevertheless, they were very largely free of vested or financial interests and shared a dedication and affection for the game of cricket. Up to the 1960s journalists, media and show-biz types, and high-profile celebrities were unthinkable and had, as yet, no place in the ranks of the Committee Room. At that time and, no doubt long before and later, an attractive perk of Committee membership was the free drinks table laid out in the Committee Room – courtesy of members' subscriptions.

As a regular minute-taker Dad delighted in surreptitiously slanting records in the direction he considered the wisest course of action. He was also wise enough to know that minutes are rarely read or ever consulted at a later date.

My mother learnt her cricket on The Roedean School playing fields overlooking the English Channel.

Soon he concluded that to be a successful committee man at Lord's you just had to ramble on longer than the opposition. He cited the much revered G O Allen, 'Gubby' to his pals, as being the great exponent of committee control and manipulation. His technique was to exasperate and exhaust any resistance to his preferred decision by interminable discourse – usually the opposition had lost the will to live or gone home. If that did not work then he referred the matter to another subcommittee (preferably one he chaired).

Latterly, Gubby Allen lived in a house at the back of the Harris Garden with a gate direct into the ground. As a confirmed bachelor, he was unashamedly wedded to his power at Lord's and no one argued with that. The only person who had his measure was my mother. At social events he expected his grand pronouncements to be received with acclamation. Whereas my mother would gently admonish him with an 'Oh, don't be so silly, Gubby!' or similar words no one else had ever dared say to him. He would visibly shrink. He might have been better prepared had he known of her very successful time at the formidable Roedean School where she had played plenty of cricket. Her no-nonsense approach on those committees would have been a breath of fresh air even though she was the nicest and most unassuming person anyone could wish to meet. Sadly, women had yet to have their day and the old brigade of committee members must now be spinning in their graves with the admission of the ladies several decades later.

REAL WORK

On a day-to-day mundane level, father was responsible for all building maintenance and minor development of Lord's buildings and estates – there was a permanent works staff of about 25 men (bricklayers, carpenters, plumbers, painters, electricians and other tradesmen) under a clerk of works, Mr Valentine. He was followed by Mr MacBeth, a quiet man and a highly skilled cabinet maker who made book cases, boxes and other items for the Dunbar family in his spare time. He was too nice to run the workforce so he and my father had a job on their hands keeping things under control – even on the move. One of the perks of the job was the immediate availability of plumbers, electricians and other trades for

Painting the sight screens.

emergencies and repairs in the home. Bill Willows, the Lord's electrician who lived in one of the Nursery End flats, looked after us way beyond the call of duty, often feeding the pets when we were on holiday and sorting out domestic chores – a delightfully kind man. When I was small his wife used to baby-sit for my parents.

The painting of the Forth railway bridge paled into insignificance compared to the annual repainting of the wooden spectator benches. Broken timbers were replaced and a third of them were renovated each winter by a team of painters. They started immediately after the last match in September, slapping paint through the winter months on miles of peeling slats which had tortured spectators' bums and backs all summer. These seats dated back to Victorian times when ergonomic comfort had yet to supersede the concept of inflicting excruciating discomfort to enhance the cricket lover's pleasure of a day at Lord's. Perhaps it was an ancient but diabolically subtle plot to make money by hiring out thousands of red and green cushions. Huge stacks of these greeted spectators on arrival at matches and on a busy day they soon disappeared. Even to this date the benches in front of the Pavilion are comfort averse.

Ground and gate control, which included stewards, commissionaires and security, was organised by Ground Superintendents who reported to my father. Dick and Joe Gaby loyally fulfilled these duties which their father had undertaken earlier in the century. Gus Farley provided ubiquitous back-up around the ground. Crowds were generally well-behaved even when not entirely sober.

Cushions for a day's spectating hired for 9d.

The lines of demarcation were often a little vague but ticket sales, membership and the accounts departments all featured somewhere in Dad's fiefdom, as did the running of the museum, library and tennis and squash courts. Nowadays, of course, there are large departments for each of these functions and more, although maybe fewer people actually watch cricket in the ground during a season. I was never told but I guess his starting salary was about £500 a year!

Audrey Jones from the Ticket Office stacks the sacks of mail to dispatch Test Match tickets in 1961.

SPECIAL LICENCE
(senseless drinking)

If all that was not enough, he inherited responsibility for running the Tavern and ground catering or, more precisely, the George Portman empire which had exercised exclusive power for some forty years. Much to father's relief George soon retired, so all catering contracts, about which Dad knew nothing, having never successfully boiled an egg in his life, fell to him, not to mention the licensing of the Lord's Tavern and all the bars around the ground. Catering companies came and went – not one mastered the vagaries of the weather and its effect on the consumption of food and drink. A full Test Match house on a hot midsummer's day would wolf down several van loads of buns, sandwiches, cakes and Wall's ice cream not to mention sinking thousands of pints of beer and other drinks. A rained off Saturday, with no cricket on Sunday, often resulted in huge quantities of food being discarded – the days of sealed wrapping had yet to dawn. Even on a good day it was hard to get things right – during a Test Match a member barged into his office to complain that the bread in the Pavilion bar sandwiches was too thick. About ten minutes later another malcontent appeared to say that the bread was meanly thin and he was still hungry. Member satisfaction at Lord's has never been an easy or smooth ride.

Lord's in the 1940s and 1950s had the privilege of a unique statutory licence to sell alcohol to the public all day long provided cricket was being or about to be played – no closing

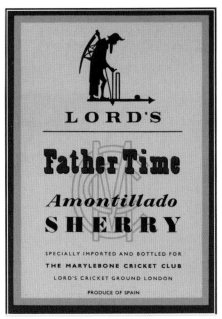

MCC marketed its own sherry to boost gate takings.

Long queues for the Gents specially between innings later on in the day.

Catering at Lords rarely went according to plan.

time until stumps were drawn. It was taken for granted that you could drink uninterrupted from mid-morning to 'stumps'. Anywhere else in the country pubs were open only for a couple of hours at lunchtime then closed for the afternoon. No doubt this legislation was passed by a Parliament riddled with MPs and peers of the old school who just happened to be MCC members. It is not a long journey from the parliamentary bars of Westminster to Lord's so a minimum interruption to their quaffing was satisfactorily achieved by our truant legislators. Spectators swayed and loafed around the Tavern all day with successive pints in hand but serious drunkenness was seldom disorderly. Any drunkenness that did occur was relatively sober and the good-natured advice offered to batsmen and other players was always precise and to the point. They were allowed real glass glasses – plastic glasses or bottles had yet to be invented and were unnecessary. The worst that ever happened was that they got dropped but use as pitch missiles was strictly for overseas tours.

ENGLAND 4 GERMANY 2

Not all the job was hard grind and one useful perk was a reciprocal arrangement with Wembley Stadium. They sent Lord's staff two tickets for their top matches and vice versa. Apart from my father, who had been a keen club footballer, no one else on the Lord's staff was too bothered about watching football so we had a dozen years of centre line seats for the FA Cup Finals and international matches. Graham Doggart and Gray, his wife, became good family friends. As an MCC Committee member and Chairman of the Football Association (1961–1963) he was a top-level link between the two leading sports of the time – cricket and football.

A pre-Olympic Tournament hockey match in 1967. India defending against Pakistan.

The ultimate experience was the 1966 World Cup final. Donald Carr, the other Assistant Secretary, found himself with two Wembley tickets and offered the spare to my father who suggested that I might like to go. We sat in the Royal Box extension two rows immediately in front of the Queen to watch England beat West Germany 4-2. We were on the centre line and Her Majesty was about three seats to one side. Billy Wright with his wife, Babs, and the other two Beverley sisters were in front of us. He spent most of the time jumping up and down blocking our view. I sat with Donald on one side and, I recall, a famous conductor, of the musical variety, on the other – possibly Sir Adrian Boult, I'm not sure. It was only years later when it gradually dawned on me what an incredibly unselfish and generous father I had been blessed with. How many people would give up a chance to watch England at home in a World Cup final, I wonder? After that day I thought England would always win. Needless to say, life's disappointment has been the ability of the English football team to perpetrate an anticlimax every four years. I kept the 1966 ticket too safely hidden; maybe I'll find it one day.

Whilst on other sports, it is not widely known that lacrosse was played regularly at Lord's. Damp winter Saturday afternoons in the 1950s saw both men's and women's matches on a pitch laid out across the far end of the ground – mostly club and university matches. Members of the public could just wander in and watch. Hockey games were also staged but in front of the Pavilion. The fixture card for these encounters fizzled out in the early 1980s with a match between Oxford and Cambridge. I suppose the Lord's slope and poor drainage were an adverse factor in winter. They were certainly unpopular with the ground staff who had to deal with cut up turf and repair the muddy damaged outfield for the coming season.

4

ABOUT THE PAVILION

LORD'S CATHEDRAL

The magnificent Long Room in the Lord's Pavilion is famous the world over but was accessible only to the privileged. MCC members, their guests and players were allowed in provided, of course, they were male. Minors under the age of eighteen, let alone eight, were strictly off limits but on a quiet moment one Sunday morning my father gave me my first glimpse of the 'holiest of holies'. Entering by one of the side-doors, this huge room opens before one, reducing self-importance to a diminutive proportion – the cathedral effect.

There have been many far more eloquent descriptions but its special attributes are twofold. First, it looks in on itself, focused by the fine, assured and lofty interior Victorian architecture of the room. In the early 1900s there were mounted antlers and big game trophy heads displayed high above the picture rails but these are long gone. Now, cricket's deep roots of tradition and history are paraded in the old paintings, mostly of country fields and players dressed in the impractical costume of their time. Stern portraits of great cricketers and personalities gaze down. Bats, balls, stumps, trophies and other simple artefacts of the game reside in glass cabinets.

The Long Room after a much needed redecoration in the early 1960s.

A view from the Long Room before the Media Centre was built.

Roy Harrington, dressing room attendant, blancoes pads and boots.

The Ashes Urn is often displayed in the Long Room.

If that is not enough, you then look outwards from the row of gigantic double-hung sash windows across the expansive panorama that is Lord's cricket ground. Facing eastwards, the Pavilion and its predecessors were positioned so the sun does not trouble the members' eyes directly. Momentarily, the studded boots of the fielding side tramping through the Long Room disturb the tranquility. The noise soon subsides as they pass through the central door and then clatter down the concrete steps onto the silence of the grass. From the other side-door the opposing batsmen follow. As soon as you start watching the cricket the room is forgotten but never for long. Sixty years ago it impressed and, now in its refurbished state, no less today.

THE THRONE OF ENGLAND

Apart from a few lady members of staff only the Queen was allowed in the Pavilion and, strictly speaking, only she could watch the cricket. This royal duty would be graciously undertaken most years, usually on a Friday, during the annual Test Match. At tea-time the England team and the visiting side lined up in front of the Pavilion to be introduced to the royal visitor. My father was in charge of, amongst other things, the seating arrangements in the Committee Room where she was entertained by the all male committee – little wonder Her Majesty has always preferred the horses.

The Committee Room chairs were allegedly rather uncomfortable or specially designed for the wrong shaped backsides. So a commodious chair

1964 : The Queen and Prince Philip meet the England and Australian teams introduced by Lord Cobham and Ted Dexter .

had to be found every year. Hence, my mother lost her desk seat at home, which was ceremoniously removed from our sitting room to be the Monarch's throne for the afternoon. I feel proud to still own what was once a temporary throne of England.

Prince Philip often slipped up to Lord's for net practice in the summer. Dad had to make sure the arrangements went smoothly and they were on familiar terms. Once he 'bumped into Philip at a Buck House Garden Party'. In conversation the Prince suggested that my father should take a handful of the chamomile lawn they were standing on as 'it grew very well'. He was right and in a few years it had spread over several square yards of our front garden lawn. Unfortunately, the ground staff lads who mowed the grass during the summer months zapped the chamomile with a selective weed killer and transformed it into our royal bald patch.

OFFICES WITH A VIEW

When my father started at Lord's he had a rather grand office room behind two large windows at the side of the Pavilion. He had a fine first floor view towards everyone entering the ground through the Grace Gates. Sitting at his desk he could see exactly who had come and gone all day long. Now this fine room has been relegated to a kitchen for the Lord's catering department. The Secretary was secreted in a pokey adjoining room with a less interesting vista overlooking the Harris Garden.

View from J G Dunbar's first office towards the Grace Gates.

Later, Dad moved to an even more spacious room on the floor immediately above the home side dressing room. Now it is a members' bar. In one corner there is a small round window from which he had an amazing view of the ground and the score on the Tavern board. In fairness to him, he was always busy, rarely watched the cricket, never knew the score and often did not know which teams were playing. In the left corner of the office was a small door to a narrow balcony with five chairs. It was once used as the radio commentary box, but when the media moved to the Press Box on the other side of the Pavilion it became the unofficial staff viewing position, especially for the lady secretaries.

MCC traditionally had a reputation for the misogynistic exclusion of women as members. However, the female staff working in the Pavilion always seemed to enjoy a relaxed and friendly relationship with their male bosses, quite a number of whom would have been utterly lost without their secretaries and personal assistants. The highest rank was gained by Diana Rait Kerr, daughter of the Colonel, who, as curator, ran the Museum and art collection in a formidable style. Behind the scenes was a family atmosphere between staff and lasting friendships flourished especially amongst the ladies. These have endured and I am told there is an annual reunion at Lord's and includes Pat (Tricia) Butterfield, Sue Bolitho, Jayne Dimmick, Gill Durrell, Jennifer Hazelden, Carol Heaton, Steph Lawrence, Veronica Lloyd, Sue McLoughlin, Thea Price, Bonnie Sills and Marnie White. Although they meet during the cricket season not much spectating takes place but this is well compensated for by the uninhibited laughter. My mother always said 'if you want anything done at Lord's ask Steph' – she worked as PA to a succession of Secretaries and knew Lord's inside out. Gill Durrell worked for my father and was an avid Hampshire supporter. She rented a flat in Primrose Hill over the Bistro

42, which later became Conrad's, with the entrance to her place through the restaurant. After play, evening diners would be startled by a large squad of the Hampshire team plus sundry hangers-on marching through the bewildered customers to the party upstairs.

At the end of the season the last, but unpublicized, and most needle match of all, was The Secretary's Eleven against the Rest of The Staff Eleven. The teams were, believe it or not, mixed, in every sense including gender and ability, and they played out on the centre of the square. Ex-Test Match playing staff adapted their game for others who knew not one end of a bat from the other. Assorted apparel was cheerfully accepted with the younger lady staff members often sporting England or county colours – any item of kit that was left in the changing rooms at the end of the season was commandeered. If I remember rightly, ladies could not be out first ball and both over and under-arm bowling were allowed. MCC was free to change the Laws whenever it decreed! The matches were usually close-run contests often deviously manipulated by outrageous umpiring decisions. Everyone had fun. Eventually, the match was relegated to the Nursery Ground and in the questionable cause of progress has long since been axed, at least in its original light-hearted form.

TENNIS ROYAL OR REAL

Located immediately behind the Pavilion, Lord's has one of the finest Real or Royal Tennis courts of some 25 surviving throughout the British Isles. The game at Lord's has thrived over the years – opening times when father took on the administration were, I think, from ten in the morning to seven in the evening; now it starts at 7am and finishes at 10 at night. What a fantastic game when played by the strong and fit professionals with awesome skill, speed and cunning. Spectators can watch from the end gallery, known as the dedans, only a few feet from the players at the service end, giving a unique close-up view of the intricacies of the game. The balls are solid, being slightly heavier but smaller than a lawn tennis ball, and sets of about thirty are made by the pros at Lord's. There is a cork centre with successive layers of cloth wound with twine and a felt cover stitched on – all done by hand. The racquet is still wood but with a thicker handle, frame and strings all necessary to resist the weight and speed of the ball.

I am told that Roger Federer was once enticed onto the Real Tennis court at the Queen's Club. The plotters assumed that holding a real tennis racket might be a tricky new experience, rendering one of the world's greatest

My first real tennis racket, 1961.

49

exponents of lawn tennis a trifle befuddled, even inept. On the contrary he stroked the skidding ball effortlessly back over the net from his first shot and never looked back– a real natural.

The game is also a refuge for the sportsman of advancing years who can adopt the game when his prowess wanes in other sports. Real Tennis offers a near lifetime of gentle or not so gentle competition but always enjoyment and camaraderie. Once the mystical scoring system is mastered, and it usually takes a few hours on court, it is utterly addictive over all other sports, even those with a stringed racket – squash and lawn tennis are relegated in the mind to the pedestrian.

Over the years there has been talk of building another court but even with all its land, sadly, MCC has yet to meet this aspiration. My inauspicious Real Tennis career began as a teenager but never improved beyond a lowly handicap of about 55. I did, however at the age of 61, win a geriatrics competition, the W H Ollis Cup, in 2004, so my name is now emblazoned on a board somewhere in the dingy corridor behind the court's 'Last Gallery'.

The old Real Tennis Court originally on the Mound Stand site.

Royal or Real Tennis at Lord's

Stages of the ball manufacture.

The core of the ball is bound with successive layers of cloth.

CLOCKWISE FROM ABOVE LEFT:
A young David Cull recovering Real Tennis balls with strips of white felt; From the dedans a set of balls delivered to the service end.; Henry Johns stringing a racket; The overhead service along the pent house; Henry Johns demonstrates the backhand grip.

The present day court in the 1950s.

ON AND OFF THE FIELD

The culture and demeanour of those who play cricket at Lord's and, for that matter, elsewhere, or administer the organisation, are unrecognisable from a few decades ago. Thankfully, once through those gates into Lord's the outside world can be forgotten for a few hours. The ever-present constant is the atmosphere – on the big match day a buzz of excitement rises from spectators intensely absorbed. On a quiet day, with a handful of watchers, the sound of a well-middled shot echoes around the stands with an assuring clarity and resonance. Without cricket, even on a dark drizzly winter's evening, the deserted Lord's retains an aloof character and atmosphere of calm superiority.

Peter May allows me to hold his trophy from the Cricket Writers' Club for the Best Young Cricketer in 1951.

The post-war game relied largely on the 'Players', professionals, who were the backbone of the first class county and international teams. A smattering of 'Gentlemen', usually ex-public school and Oxbridge, captained teams and acted as a socially acceptable link through the hierarchy. On scorecards and records the amateurs always had their initials before their surnames, for example, W G Grace, whereas the 'pros' were recorded with initials after, like Trueman F S. I often wonder how WG would have fared against the likes of modern day 'Truemen'; not very well, particularly on some of the 19th century Lord's wickets, I suspect.

The Gentlemen were amateurs who, at least in theory, were not paid for their services to their county or country. Either they had private means or latterly were retained by lenient employers who relied on the public relations value of their gentleman players. For example, take the three great amateur batsmen of the 1950s. Peter May was an insurance broker in the City and David Sheppard was the first ordained priest to play for England, whereafter he journeyed northwards to become Bishop of Liverpool and sat as a labour peer in the House of Lords. Colin Cowdrey led a versatile life of good work and causes for which he was awarded a CBE, a Knighthood and Peerage. The social distinctions and culture at Lord's were deeply engrained and perhaps their gradual erosion has yet to fade totally into oblivion. At least by the time of our arrival at Lord's the custom of the Gentlemen and Players taking the field from different pavilion doors had been abolished.

Lord's always had a reputation for conservative tradition and being aloof from the real world but the truth is surprisingly different. In fact, it should be recalled that, with the exception of ping-pong, MCC was the first major sporting administration to abolish formally the distinction between amateur and professional players. The longstanding and prestigious Gentlemen v Players match was a highlight of the season's fixture card and attracted good crowds. Abolition in 1963 was, perhaps, the very first step in the modernisation of the game and a blow to the ludicrous class divisions in cricket. Football, tennis and other sports followed but fusty old cricket had led the way.

MEMBERSHIP – A LONG WAIT

Amongst cricket lovers, MCC membership is a much sought-after and coveted privilege. Membership opens up a whole world of entitlements – free entry into Lord's and the Pavilion for all matches, priority for ticket applications, the opportunity to play for the club at a level suitable to your ability, net practice and coaching, access to Real Tennis, dinners and social events, golf and bridge and plenty more.

The popular demand has from time to time resulted in a near lifetime's wait before election, but over the years the club has devised ways of shortening the process. In 1963 money was needed, so several thousand associate members were 'created' and I was lucky enough to be caught by the new intake. At the same time a fearsome increase of 50% in membership subscriptions was imposed from £6 to £9 per annum. Of course, the full annual subscription is now pushing £500. Apart from being excluded from the Pavilion for Test

Even in the dead of winter etiquette must be observed!

Matches and one or two major events, there was little difference between associate and full membership. Still only in my early twenties, I gained the latter only a few years later thanks to another substantial increase in the numbers.

Of course, a quicker route now to membership is by playing qualifying matches, which seems a much more appropriate route for joining the great club. It used to be quite easy; by choosing modest opposition from the huge fixture list of the MCC's non-first class games each season, full membership might be achieved in three years. Buy your captain a drink or two to secure a favourable report, don't drop catches off his bowling, score a few runs and you were home and dry.

Gradually the authorities have implemented a complicated system for the proposal and eventual election of candidates. This includes a strangely nepotic nomination process apparently to weed out undesirables or avoid a dissident members' coup d'état.

Now, to be a playing member, you are expected to produce elaborate records of your cricketing prowess – including batting and bowling averages, run rates, economy, blah blah, etcetera – but nothing about whether or not you walk having quietly snicked a ball to the wicket-keeper. Now the question is whether or not you have the bottle not to walk when you know perfectly well that you are out. Regrettably, the attempted bolting of the Pavilion doors came long after Sky and the estuarine sharp suits, not to mention the coloured track ones, had barged a well-worn path to the inner sanctums of the game. If more playing members were to be stipulated in the Rules, Marylebone would diminish such problems and also be a proper Cricket Club.

The free seats on a big match day.

5

CRICKET WATCHING

MY VIEWS

The whole point of Lord's is cricket playing and watching. Early on during our first summer at Lord's my mother discovered I could not read the scoreboard from across the ground. I was promptly dispatched to the optician who was amazed that, with such awful short sight, I even knew where the scoreboard was. Soon I was kitted out with national health wire-rimmed 'gig-lamps' (as my father described them) and a whole new world magically appeared before me. One eye was so bad as to be near useless but, unlike the great batsman, the Nawab of Pataudi, who only had sight in one eye, it turned out to be an additional handicap to my modest sporting abilities. Fortunately, if you enjoy doing something it doesn't matter so much how well or incompetently you do it.

Successive MCC Secretaries, the Colonel, Ronnie Aird and Billy Griffith, had a box in the old Grand Stand, the lower one nearest the Pavilion end, and generously allowed my mother and me to use it for all matches, except I was banished when VIPs were being entertained which usually only happened during Test Matches. I then had to sit on a small patch of grass between the A Stand and the Pavilion Press Box which was roped off from the public – exclusive but less comfortable. As a special treat I was occasionally installed in the Tavern scorebox to 'help', somewhat of a euphemism for keeping out of

Watching cricket can be exhausting – in the shadow of the free seats.

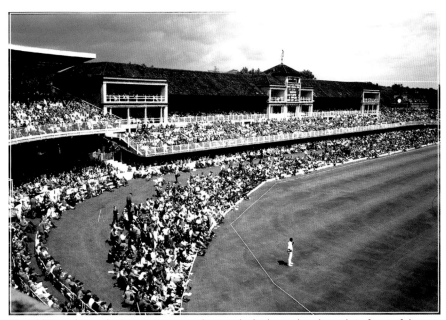

The old Grand Stand – Spectators crowd towards the boundary boards in front of the Grand Stand partly obscured by the upper tier of the Warner Stand. The Secretary's box was on the left hand side on the lower level.

The Grand Stand scoreboard with the scorer's box over – probably the best bird's eye view of the ground for cricket watching.

Jim Sims, Middlesex and England 1929–1952, in the scorer's box.

the way. The total and batsmen's scores were on large revolving numbered wheels which had to be turned when a run was scored. All other numbers for wickets, bowlers, fall of last wicket, etcetera were displayed on metal plates which had to be slid in and out of the appropriate window slots. Pandemonium would break out on the fall of a wicket as numbers had to be changed all over the board. Finding the right metal plates was a real test and another quick wicket generated some fresh language. If the two scoreboards did not tally, frantic phone calls were exchanged across the ground. The crowd was never slow or shy about pointing out an error.

The Grand Stand scorebox used canvas loops to display the scores which were controlled by the scorers sitting above.

Meanwhile, the Secretaries' wives were enlisted to socialise with guests during these matches as their husbands were usually much too busy being men in the Pavilion. My mother, Barbara Griffith, Stella Carr and other wives played a key role chatting up diverse assortments of cricket dignitaries. Their social skills, diplomacy and charm won them many friends from home and overseas, all of whom enjoyed their day at Lord's.

CROWDS BEFORE DAWN AND BOUNDARY BOARDS

The Lord's corner with the Wellington and St John's Wood Roads is often where spectators get their first glimpse of the ground when walking from Baker Street or the Regent's Park direction. Part of the outer wall has a fine frieze by Gilbert Bayes, RA, of cricketers, a golfer, footballer, rower, athlete and other sportsmen. Erected in 1934, it occupies a diagonal position across the corner. Originally under the figures was the famous inscription carved in the stone 'Play up, play up and play the game'. Mysteriously, these great words disappeared during a renovation and now only appear in barely legible small lettering on the frieze. Maybe this innovation was a recognition that the spirit of the game has evolved and batsmen now never walk until the umpire raises a finger or Hawkeye condemns. The high minded sculptor would be horrified that ruthless ethics now dominate the game.

I remember vividly the enthusiasm of the Test Match watching public of the 1950s which gradually subsided in the next decade or two. Pre-bought tickets were few and far between; you

The boundary rope.

just had to turn up, queue and pay for entrance. Those prepared to miss a night's sleep to keep a place at the front of the queue were rewarded in that, once in the ground, there were the 'free seats'(rebuilt as the Compton and Edrich Stands) – first come, first served at the Nursery End. When all the seats had gone the less lucky spectators could sit on the grass behind a low wooden boundary board.

Wooden boards, about nine inches high, were staked into the ground just behind the boundary rope to contain the masses and were reasonably well respected. Behind the boards spectators sat on the grass but, with a full house, arms and legs gradually intruded onto the field of play. Stewards patrolled to admonish these limbs which obediently retreated only to return once the danger had passed by. With a capacity crowd so close to the pitch, the buzz and atmosphere in the ground was always exciting, regardless of what the cricket was like. The grass spectators made Lord's look full but also intimate and intense.

To get a good position the ticketless queued all night and by six o'clock in the morning the Lord's block would be surrounded by an expectant queue nearly a mile long. This shuffled past our front gate in Elm Tree Road towards the North Gate. We never complained about the queues or crowds going to and from the ground – in fact it was always rather exciting. Serious traffic jams were short-lived and rarely inconvenient for us locals.

Preparing the pitch – the heavy roller pulled by a ground staff squad under the supervision of Headgroundsman, Ted Swannell (right).

A MATCH REMEMBERED

West Indian supporters of this time were famously exuberant, often to the point of frenzy. Standing three or four deep at the back of the free seats they roared encouragement in a crescendo of noise as their fast bowlers charged in. Wes Hall and Charlie Griffiths were the main protagonists and the darlings of their supporters. A forest of jumping bodies and gesticulating arms attempted to distract and intimidate some unfortunate, no doubt, inwardly trembling English batsman. The crowd loved a good thump in the ribs or some other more delicate part of the anatomy and if the ball hit the stumps as well, even better – it was all very good-natured, I think!

To me the most memorable match at Lord's was the West Indies Test Match in 1963. It was touch and go as to which team might win and, as Wisden said, four results were possible by the last over – England requiring 6 runs with 9 wickets down. The climax had built as England struggled for the runs and lost wickets. The West Indian bowlers controlled the last hour's play by completing a mere eight overs. Wes Hall, one of the finest, most athletic fast bowlers ever, started his run-up just short of the Pavilion steps, reaching his mark in an almost motionless amble. At the Nursery End, Griffiths, less elegant but equally ferocious, was contemplating having the sightscreen moved so it would not block his run-up. Since it was the last day, the ground was practically empty. Earlier in the second innings Colin Cowdrey broke his arm but had returned heroically, arm in plaster, to the crease when the penultimate wicket fell. As history records, it ended as a draw which was accepted as the fairest finish – cricket is never boring, it just takes time!

Exuberant West Indian supporters cheer on their fast bowlers.

*Harry Sharp, all-rounder for Middlesex
1946–1957.*

*Jack Robertson, opening batsman for
Middlesex and England 1937–1959.*

Judi Doull from New Zealand.

*Peter Parfitt, all-rounder and fine slip fielder
for Middlesex and England 1956–1972.*

Fast bowlers at Lord's

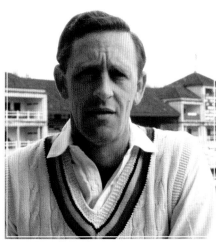

Brian Statham, fast bowler for Lancashire
and England at Lord's for his last Test Match.

Bill Voce, medium fast bowler for
Notts and England 1927–1952.

Freddie Trueman, fast bowler for Yorkshire
and England 1949–1969.

Fred Trueman

MIDDLESEX HEROES

Middlesex County Cricket Club, whose premier home ground was Lord's, had Denis Compton, and his elder brother Leslie, Bill Edrich, Jack Robertson, Fred Titmus, Jim Simms, John Warr, Alan Moss and a succession of other wonderful players, some of who played for England. Getting home from school gave time to watch the last hour of play which always finished at 6.30 – no rules about minimum over rates or anything like that.

Denis Compton was, of course, one of my heroes and his achievements are well recorded in the annals of cricket history. The leg sweep may not quite have been his invention but his mastery of batting enabled him to play this dangerously tricky shot sparingly and usually successfully. It was not entirely appreciated by the purists of his time as it broke all the coaching rules about playing straight and not crossing the line of the ball. Not until several decades later do we see the reverse sweep, the scoop and other innovative batting techniques being perfected though often with disastrous consequences in the bowler's favour. Compton would, I think, have enjoyed developing new skills to master unorthodox ways of scoring runs and frustrating the fielding captain's attempts at effective field placing. His career was blighted by a troublesome bad knee, an operation for which put him out of

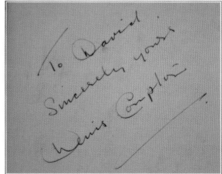

Denis Compton prolific run scorer for Middlesex and England.

action for a good six months. With modern day key-hole surgery he would be back only few weeks later. Off the field he was a familiar face on advertising hoardings across the country, encouraging every young man to become more handsome by grooming his hair with the essential Brylcreem.

WHAT A DRAG, CHUCK

During the 1960s there was an increasing concern that bowlers were gaining an unfair advantage over batsmen. Put simply, fast bowlers were delivering the ball from some seventeen or eighteen yards from the batsman which was considered too close bearing in mind the ball was propelled at speeds of up to about ninety miles an hour. This was achieved by a massive delivery stride with the front foot landing well in front of the popping crease. The back foot was dragged from where it landed, legally, behind the bowler's crease to a point well in front of that crease. There was a gathering of the great and good on the Nursery Ground – Sir Pelham Warner, Gubby Allen, Harry Altham, Freddie Brown, Trevor Bailey, MCC Secretaries, and other cricket luminaries along with a collection of contemporary fast bowlers. Their actions, in particular their footwork, was filmed in slow motion and scrutinised minutely by the assembled company.

Frank Tyson demonstrated his foot placing by bowling flat out, and still photos taken by my father show that the point of release was at least a yard in front of the popping crease. The deliberations eventually resulted in amendments to the Laws of Cricket to the effect that the bowler's front foot had to land wholly or partially behind the popping crease. The ball's release was, therefore, prevented from being too far forward. All this was rather technical and boring but the change in the Law had a profound effect on all bowlers, especially the quickies and continues satisfactorily to this day.

A few years earlier the Law-makers had been faced with the problem of bowlers throwing or chucking the ball to gain extra speed against batsmen. I well remember the South African fast bowler Geoff Griffin who was no-balled consistently in the second Test Match at Lord's in 1960 and a later exhibition match. Incidentally his action was also a clear example of the 'drag'. The difficulty of identifying a throw still exercises the authorities even with the advantages of very high speed slow motion cameras. Lasith Malinga from

Analysing the fast bowler – Frank Tyson demonstrates the 'drag'.

Sri Lanka, the very successful and old-fashioned round-arm bowler or slinger, has given both umpires and batsmen serious headaches with his flailing arms 'bowling' action. After lengthy international scrutiny this unique action has, however, been deemed legitimate, so at least that one was resolved.

A CHANCE IN THE GOOD OLD DAYS

I recently discovered an old scorecard of the 1950s which shows how cricket watching opportunities have diminished. On the back were the season's fixtures which showed Lord's hosted well over 100 days cricket in a season. And they never, quite rightly in my view, played on a Sunday. Almost every day from late April Middlesex CCC played all their three-day county championship home matches there. Schools, the services, MCC, and other teams all played there. Nowadays, there are fewer than half the number of cricket days. It was, and still is, the dream of every cricketer, however great or useless, to play at Lord's and they had a better chance then. Lord's gave all English cricketers an incentive and spirit for the game. A few achieved an enviable memory of maybe scoring a run, a century, or taking a wicket, a hat trick – but just as memorably the agony of collecting a duck or dropping a catch! It did not matter; you had played at Lord's.

Until the advent of limited overs matches the annual touring side had a very long and, no doubt, wearying fixture list. This consisted of five five-day Test Matches, three-day games against most or all the first class county sides, Oxford and Cambridge, Minor Counties, MCC and probably one or two other encounters. The quick bowlers frequently clocked up 30 overs in a day which would be an impressive feat of stamina especially if sustained

View from the Pavilion balcony on a quiet day but still a pleasure to watch the cricket.

The first floodlit match at Lord's with Middlesex v. Derbyshire, 10th September 2007.

throughout a season. More recently the night-match floodlights have been installed, resulting in a somewhat fragile relationship between local residents, Westminster City Council and Lord's. On the grounds of light 'pollution' the Council have goaded themselves into imposing restrictions. As matches are usually finished by dusk and Lord's has been there for nearly 200 years it all calls for sensible tolerance and acceptance.

At the end of play in most matches the square would be roped off and spectators permitted to promenade on the ground to inspect the pitch. After a long hot day, the battlefield, that narrow strip of hard, dry, dusty, near grassless earth, presented a close-up opportunity for infinite conjecture, comment and debate. To stand in the middle of the ground is an extraordinary sensation of almost limitless space, a panorama, and far more impressive than the view from any stand. The playing area is larger than needed for a single match so the stands are a long distance from the players and visually shrink away. In a curious way I think the famous slope across the ground slightly opens the horizon to give an even greater feeling of space. It is awe-inspiring and no wonder every cricketer wants to play at Lord's.

POSH BOYS BEHAVING DISGRACEFULLY

On the whole, spectators have always been very well behaved and orderly. Much the worst exception to this was once after an Eton and Harrow match. The winning team, I can't remember which, hung a long banner over the edge of the dressing room balcony and wastefully squirted champagne over the gathering crowd below. The losing side spectators took serious umbrage, climbed over the fence at the front of the Pavilion and tried to tear down the

Eton v. Harrow - Top Hats and Tails

CLOCKWISE FROM TOP: *Coaches on the Tavern concourse; Inspecting the wicket – lunchtime promenade on the ground.; Reminiscing about previous encounters, perhaps; Coaches arrived on lorries and commandeered for spectating but largely for drinking and falling asleep in.*

Spectators at the Eton v. Harrow match.

offending banner. Fire extinguishers were commandeered to repel the invaders, as were beer mugs, cushions and other assorted missiles. Ungentlemanly scuffles ensued between the young 'gentleman' supporters from the two schools. Fists were banging dangerously on the large glass windows of the Long Room. I caught a glimpse of my father behind one. Anarchy was taking hold. Rude words were noisily exchanged. The young men cascaded over the benches and each other. A couple of bewildered looking policemen eventually appeared. The rioters lost their nerve and suddenly melted away – and a more decorous calm settled almost instantly. Unlike the Alamo, the Pavilion did not fall but there was a nasty moment or two until they slunk off to their ancestral estates.

BOMBS AWAY

An entertaining occasion occurred during a Test Match when a bomb threat was 'phoned to the ground. An announcement came over the loudspeaker system for everyone to leave Lord's immediately. The players sat down on the square and the spectators were not budging. Eventually they left the field and the crowd, who didn't take kindly to their pleasure being interrupted, sauntered out. I was in the Q Stand and wandered home to find about 200 of our friends and acquaintances, not to mention their friends as well, all sprawled out on our back lawn – refugees from Lord's, all expecting a cup of tea and cucumber sandwiches! Fortunately, the police only found empty beer glasses so the cricket resumed quite quickly as the massed hordes waiting outside the Grace Gates were getting restless. Their interest was cricket, not bombs!

A WAY OF LIFE

Our proximity to the action in Lord's enabled us to hear the five minute bell sounded to herald the start of play at the beginning of the day, or resumption after an interval or the start of a new innings. Rung vigorously the sound could easily be heard throughout our house. The sounding of the bell by an umpire or the pavilion staff warned spectators to return to their seats if they did not want to miss the cricket. Over the years this quaint theatrical ritual has evolved, on occasions, into a more ceremonial event. The ringing of the bell has been an honour afforded to distinguished, usually retired, players and other celebrities known for their enthusiasm for the game.

Being so close to the stands the crowd sounds on a big match day could be a commentary in their own right, particularly during a needle Test Match. One soon learnt from the seclusion of the garden or indoors, that different noises were a clear indication of what dramas were being played out over the wall. A very sudden loud roar, then cheering and clapping usually meant that an important opposition, preferably Australian, batsman had been bowled or smartly caught. A catch, depending on how far the ball had to travel, was slightly different with some shouting before the ball was actually caught then a similar noise sequence. A batsman returning to the Pavilion with an ignominiously small score or a duck might receive a sympathetic ripple of applause, barely audible, as he made his way, head down, up the Pavilion steps. An initial cheer and a more sustained level of applause greets a batsman's century.

Our home had rapidly become a magnet for my parents' cricketing friends who soon discovered easy access to and from the ground through our back garden. A few days before major matches the phone would start ringing with those (members only, of course) wanting

A steward rings the five minute bell warning the ground of an imminent battle in the middle.

Umpire, Syd Buller taking the field.

A 'king pair' of mallard ominously inspect the wicket!

to park their cars in our limited space driveway. Close of play heralded an influx of thirsty spectators who had to be revived with gins and tonics, sherries and beers. Often we hosted fifty or sixty guests for post-Test Match evening drinks – amongst whom there was often a sprinkling of players, MCC Committee members and overseas visitors.

Bed and breakfast was also a regular service for some cricketing visitors attending dinners and meetings at Lord's. Harry Altham, Winchester school master and eminent cricket guru, was always welcome, particularly as he shared with my father a strong interest in coaching and youth cricket and we all talked well into the night. In retrospect, it occurs to me that my parents only asked people they liked to stay and, commendably, never had an ulterior motive of career advancement for my father.

A SIDEWAYS WICKET

It has always been taken for granted that wickets at Lord's go roughly east to west or vice versa – in other words end to end in a line from the Pavilion to the Nursery Ground. The only exception seems to have been when Peter May made a coaching film for batting in the mid-1950s. For some reason, possibly to do with the light from the sun's angle, a pitch was laid out across the hallowed square. My father volunteered me for ball retrieving and I was posted just in front of the Grand Stand fence. My orders were 'Don't try to stop the ball – just roll them back after they hit the fence'. I remember thinking this was rather wimpish advice.

The cameras rolled and Peter effortlessly performed his elegant but ferocious straight and cover drives at me stationed some fifty yards away. Even though

Batting Masterclass – Peter May and Colin Cowdrey

Peter May, balanced stance.

Colin Cowdrey, immaculate straight back-lift.

Impenetrable forward defensive.

Cover drive.

Leg glance.

Square cut.

facing up the slope the time delay between the ball leaving the bat and it thwacking into the boundary fence seemed like a fraction of a second – a bullet skidding over the grass. Not relishing the loss of a few fingers, if not an entire hand or two, I had no hesitation in obeying instructions. I scuttled out of their way and henceforth felt great sympathy for any fielder who ever had to face May's driving. Peter May and Colin Cowdrey displayed their batting skills for another coaching film. My father took the opportunity to record their efforts and a few of his pictures feature on the masterclass page.

Father like son, Chris Cowdrey, in the Easter Classes.

SECOND LORD'S SITE

The Regent's Canal linking Paddington's Grand Canal to Camden cut through the second site of Lord's Cricket Ground in 1813. The Ground was located on the lefthand bend necessitating the move to the current site in St John's Wood a year later. In the early nineteenth century John Nash designed exclusive villas along the north and south canal banks. These gradually fell into disrepair and the estates made way for a power station and the vast Marylebone railway goods yard in 1900. In turn the yard was cleared for redevelopment as Council housing in the 1960s. Beyond the levelled land are two familiar London landmarks on the horizon - the 627 foot high Post Office Tower (to the right of the picture and now known as the BT Tower) topped out in 1964 and the 36 floor Euston Tower (centre) completed in 1970.

The Regent's Canal cut through the site of the second Lord's Cricket Ground.

6

AROUND THE GROUND

R STAND?

With the passage of time almost unimaginable changes have evolved on the Lord's landscape, that is to say the modernisation of its stands, buildings and facilities and, more recently, electronic scoreboards, replay screens and floodlights. Only The Pavilion and Q Stand, now the Allen Stand, remain substantially the same but with radical improvements. Stands or sections, as in the Grand and Mound Stands, were designated alphabetically from the A Stand, north of the Pavilion, round the ground to Q Stand to the south. The Pavilion might in theory have been known as the R Stand. 'Let's take a walk around the ground', as my father used to say.

Left to right, the original Lord's Tavern, Tavern Stand, the clock Tower Stand & Boxes and 'Q' Stand.

RED HOT GERANIUMS

Lord's employed two gardeners, Messrs Stanhope and Spalding, as already mentioned. They were housed in two large wooden framed greenhouses surrounded by cold frames probably dating back to Victorian times. These were sited on an area of open, slightly rural, land on the corner of St John's Wood Road where the big block of flats, Century Court, now stands. The dominant flora were healthy weeds, thistles, willow herb and stinging nettles, vigorously nurtured by the gardeners' neglect. Before World War II there were also greenhouses at the back of the A Stand adjoining the back garden of number 8 Elm Tree Road.

However, one great talent of the gardeners was propagating pillar-box red geraniums for the Harris Gardens and other flowerbeds scattered around Lord's. Between long periods of hibernation they had brief, but hectic, pre-cricket season planting and autumn clearing sessions but otherwise were rarely seen away from their warm retreat. On their retirement, Clifton Nurseries took over the horticultural duties and a block of flats, Century Court, and the new Tavern block obliterated a peaceful little green enclave. On the same corner there is a small flat slab of concrete surrounded by a dwarf brick wall. Apparently this covers a 100 foot deep shaft to some subterranean watercourse, one of London's ancient rivers.

The Harris Garden was for many years the traditional location for team photographs, which were invariably taken on the practice day – the day before the start of the match. Many of the England team pictured at Lord's on Wednesday 17th June 1959 would have played for their counties until the previous evening, leaving only the Wednesday available for nets, interviews, photographs and general preparation.

CORONATION PLEA FROM WG

The back garden of 12 Grove End Road gives picnickers a pleasant space as it now forms part of the Coronation Garden, the simple layout for which was designed by my father. The two cast iron urns in the Coronation Garden were salvaged from the old garden of number twelve. Partially an outdoor museum, various Lord's artefacts reside there, although periodically they do get moved around, including the statue of W G Grace, an antique turnstile and the big roller. The latter, weighing five tons, had not been used for some years and was to be discarded for scrap metal but Dad intervened so that it eventually became a museum piece. During Dr Beeching's era of railway rationalisation, or should one say massacre, the 'Thomas Lord' plaque was rescued from a redundant railway steam engine. No one at Lord's knew what to do with it so a few bolts on the roller engineered a happy marriage with said plaque. At least half a dozen ground staff had been needed to propel it, and the other problem the roller caused was a depression at either end of the wicket. When it was slowed down to be reversed weight was exerted for longer in the batting and stump areas.

Statue of W G Grace in the Coronation Garden with Thomas Lord, the redundant five ton roller – two heavyweights of their time.

At the centre of the far lawn the ancient willow, with its York stone paved circle, remains where it has grown for over a hundred years, witnessing many secrets. Just above head height the trunk divides upwards into a tortured tangle of branches. Today's Test Match picnickers don't give it a second glance – maybe they will now. The high brick wall behind the old turnstiles has a small gap at ground level now filled with some loose bricks and blocked on the other side by some flats. This enabled our cat to get from our back garden into Lord's without having to scale any heights.

It has to be said that WG's shady corner of exile in the Coronation Garden is not really befitting to possibly the most eminent cricketer of all times. Umpire Dickie Bird's statue has been raised in his home town of Barnsley. Bobby Moore stands proudly outside Wembley Stadium. Why not a mini roundabout just inside the Grace Gates entrance with 'WG' on a plinth greeting all those who visit Lord's? There is plenty of space. His figure is instantly recognisable and imposing, even if the posed shot he is playing may be technically a little suspect.

THE OLD GRAND STAND AND PRINTING

The rear of the old Grand Stand had a warren of dusty rooms, grubby staircases and murky corridors. An airy walk-way ran under the length of the stand – at the west end the level was high enough to watch the cricket over the spectators' heads in the lower tier of seats known as B Stand. If an overseas touring side was playing, the tickets here were allocated to their supporters. With one of the two

The upper and lower cases from which the type was selected to be placed in the hot metal printing blocks. The original Heidelberg printers have long since been archived into retirement under the Mound Stand.

Grand Stand long bars immediately behind, this was always a well-fuelled, entertainingly boisterous and partisan section of the crowd.

Before the advent of the electronic scoreboards only the numbers of the players were shown on the old manual boards. Unless you were familiar with the players on each side they could only be identified by referring to a score card giving names and numbers. Lord's had its own printing press located between the two Grand Stand bars. Up-to-date cards were on sale from one of the press's latticed glass windows. Within minutes 'the fall of the last wicket' would be shown on the latest batch of cards. They would be

Score cards in the printing machine.

rushed around the ground to the points where junior members of the ground staff sold them to in-coming spectators with the chorus of 'Match card – card of the match!' – often in competition with the news-vendors' call of 'Star, News and Standard.' Three evening papers – those were the days of real choice. The printing office also produced tickets, membership bumph, dinner menus and other MCC paperwork, all from their old German Heidelberg presses. Letters were selected from two cases – capitals from the upper case, or open tray, and lower, and set into the printing blocks of hot metal. Once computers and digital printing took over the old presses were archived under the Mound Stand.

Upstairs in the Grand Stand there were dining rooms for the seventeen boxes which each accommodated about a dozen spectators. The painted brick walls were shabby, the windows filthy frosted glass and the concrete floors grimy – there was little incentive for diners to eat, let alone enjoy, their lunches and afternoon teas in such surroundings bordering on squalid. The only consolation was that the side-on view of the pitch from the boxes, and the upper balcony, was brilliant. However, seated at either side of the upper covered area, part of the ground was visually obscured. The balcony seats below also blocked sight of the near boundary.

TWENTIETH CENTURY MAKEOVER

The replacement by the new stand in 1998 was a welcome improvement for spectators. Regrettably, the architects failed to maintain a dignified resting place for Father Time on his traditional perch atop the old Grand Stand. So he now faces the wind in an altogether less prominent roost on the other side of the ground – such relegation has, of course, failed to slow his march.

The old Grand Stand 1926–1996.

In the dead of winter, early 1950s, Father Time was removed temporarily for cleaning and repair. David makes a close inspection.

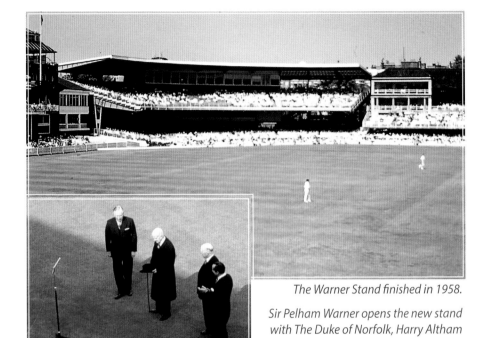

The Warner Stand finished in 1958.

Sir Pelham Warner opens the new stand with The Duke of Norfolk, Harry Altham and Ronnie Aird.

Since our arrival at Lord's the ground has seen major changes although the general ambience and atmosphere is surprisingly and reassuringly of the old tradition. The magnificent Pavilion, which has been preserved and sensibly modernised, is the architectural heart and soul of Lord's. In sporting terms it is as symbolic of cricket as Big Ben or the Tower of London are to the Nation. Every decade or so, one of the surrounding functional stands will succumb to their transient existence and be knocked down for redevelopment but the Pavilion remains, one hopes, forever.

After the War the first to go, as already mentioned, was the A Stand to be replaced by the Warner Stand named after one of the great Lord's stalwarts. The grey metal work and concrete, to last at least a hundred years, brought a new modern design to the ground. The press and commentary facilities were moved from the small Pavilion extension, now the Chief Executive's office, to the more extensive facilities in the new stand. They were not popular as the view was at an unhelpfully side-on angle to the wicket. There was inevitable conflict between committee and some members who objected to spending the money or to the design, but usually both. For the next fifty years any proposal to redevelop a part of the ground has met with minority howls of protest often followed by Special General Meetings, committee censures and much hot air. It is fair to say that the eventual outcomes have been good compromises for the club with all the warring sides contentedly licking their wounds in the happy belief that they were right. The good thing, now considered a defect, about the Warner Stand is that the seats are generously spaced with plenty of legroom. This almost condemns the stand for imminent redevelopment, along Monarch Airlines design criteria, with seats jammed together to cram in many more bums and increase spectator numbers.

The demolition of the old Tavern and the Clock Tower and Stand and the loss of its bar and concourse from which one could stand and watch the cricket was a dent in the ground's spirit. More cynically, it was the first concession to the money men wanting to place more bums on paid-for seats. The seriously uninspirational concept and design of the new 'Lord's Tavern', not even overlooking the ground, was an opportunity which slipped through the experts' fingers.

1962. The old Main Gate next to the Lord's Tavern now replaced by the Bicentenary Gate. Made of a heavy hard wood it often got stuck on its overhead runners.

Lord's Tavern from St John's Wood Road in 1963. The bakery shop is on the left and the old Main Gate to the right.

Three bar beer pulls salvaged from the demolished Tavern.

Beer barrels in the basement of the old Tavern.

Demolition of the Lord's Tavern

TOP LEFT: *The Tavern Stand's last stand – the Clock Tower also went;* TOP RIGHT: *The Tavern Bar Clock with three minutes of 'drinking up time' left before finally closing;* ABOVE: *The new Lord's Tavern site on the corner of St John's Wood and Grove End Roads;* RIGHT: *Billy Griffith, MCC Secretary, symbolically swings his pickaxe to start the demolition.*

The scoreboard is craned into a temporary position at deep extra cover while construction of the new stand commences.

The New Stand and Tavern

NEW TAVERN STAND LORD'S

Plan for the new Tavern Stand. One tier was omitted to save money

The scoreboard returns to its new perch for a while until replacement by the more informative electronic version.

Conversely, the Media Centre, growing from two concrete stalks between the Compton and Edrich Stands was an unlikely triumph of design vision and imagination. The outer skin of shining aluminium was finally riveted together by a team of ship welders from the south coast. The ironic shape of a rugby ball with a large glass mouth (attributed with some similarity to the wife of a former Prime Minister), the Media Centre is totally incongruous, creating an imposing presence and is happily accepted as part of the Lord's scene. The interior is strangely minimalist and a sort of clinical pale blue like a not very modern hospital. Luckily, it seems to be fit for purpose and, if the press do not complain, they must have got it right.

Lord's is, perhaps, at its most tranquil and embracing late on a warm summer's evening after an exciting and noisy day's cricket with a full house. Dad and I would go 'round the ground' at ten o'clock to see how the clearing up was progressing. Tons of bottles and rubbish would be piled up for the late-night refuse lorries. The teams of motley casual labour characters who queued at the North Gate before close of play to wield a broom for a quid or two in hand, aimed to finish before closing time. Gradually the sun calmly sets and the place regains a peace ready for the next day's play.

THE TAVERN AND THE SLOPE

The original Lord's Tavern overlooked the ground directly opposite the Grand Stand. Until sometime in the late 1950s there was a baker's shop next to the Tavern – all the bread was produced in a bakery a few yards away under the Mound Stand and sold deliciously fresh and warm. Quite how or why a bakery came to be within a cricket ground some other historian will have to reveal, but it probably reflects the power of the Portman catering and other enterprises empire which reigned for a good many decades before the War.

The Tavern had little architectural merit; in fact, it was antiquated, inconvenient, a health hazard, but had some tired character. The cellars supported a flourishing population of cockroaches and assorted rodents. A flat concourse enabled spectators to grab their pints and socialise whilst watching the cricket over or round the heads of others. When crowded, the viewing was not good but it never worried the drinkers. There were two ground-floor bars and a restaurant upstairs where many of the MCC dinners were held.

Just below the Tavern scorebox was a small kiosk with green shutters, the only Lord's shop, selling books, Wisdens, postcards, player photos and prints – all the cricket ephemera. The Playfair Cricket Annual was my favourite as it recorded all the previous year's matches, was nicely illustrated and more entertaining than its august rival.

The notorious Lord's 'slope' was and is real and used to be delineated on half a dozen cast iron columns which supported the old Tavern Balcony. The green paint on each column was terminated nearly seven feet up by a black circle, which indicated the level of the ground at the far side boundary by the Grand Stand.

The slope has been blamed for many a bizarre happening to batsmen arising from the ground's incline down from north to south. Legendary deviations of flight and pitch of the ball achieved by bowlers were attributed to the slope, although less so in recent years due to the slight levelling of the square. One aspect which I do not recall being mentioned by writers is the visual impact of the near seven foot drop from one side of the ground to the other. Is there any other major sporting venue which is not built around a level playing field? Hence the Grand Stand looks down on the Tavern and Mound Stands; the Pavilion shows the slope's gradient along the brick boundary line fence. Perhaps these contours in some way enhance the spectators' impression of the Lord's grandeur.

The columns' black rings supporting the Tavern balcony indicate the height of the downward slope from across the ground.

When there was no cricket being played patrons could enter the Tavern from the road and sit out at the back overlooking the ground. This was a pleasant spot on a warm summer's evening. Drinkers used to win money from their friends with an apparently easy challenge. The innocent punter was blindfolded and stood inside the boundary fence facing the Grand Stand, to which they had to walk across the field without stopping or cheating. The distance is much further than most realised and the upward slope confusing. Invariably disorientation and panic set in about a third of the way across. Onlookers offered cruelly unhelpful advice while the bewildered loser circled about for a while and, at best, ended up in front of the Pavilion or colliding into the sightscreens. For some reason most finished quite close to where they started – in front of the Tavern but never anywhere near the Grand Stand.

In 1966 my father and I had the nostalgic distinction of sharing the last pint ever pulled in the old Tavern building prior to its demolition. Next day Billy Griffith, perched precariously on a parapet wall, swung a pickaxe to dislodge the first brick of the Tavern's demise. Later that day Dad was sober enough to rescue three ceramic beer pull handles from the contractor's rubble lorry. Each had a small hand-painted vignette copied from famous paintings in the Lord's art collection – 'Grace' (A J Stuart Wortley, 1890), 'The Scorer' (Thomas Henwood, 1842) and 'Tossing for Innings' (Robert James, 1841). At the base of each handle is the figure of a hare in different cricketing poses: sitting in a deckchair waiting

84

As part of the Tavern Stand redevelopment the Grace Gates were disassembled and constructed about 10 feet to the left.

to bat, bowling and fielding, the significance of which escapes me. A skilful cabinetmaker, Mr MacBeth, who was on the works staff, turned wooden bases to convert them into sedate table-lamps of unique cricket drinking history.

THE BIG GREEN MOUND

The old A Stand, between the Pavilion and Grand Stand, was a single storey concrete quarter circle with about a dozen rows of freestanding benches and a corrugated iron roof. It had a friendly feel, which may explain why it was immortalised by the G H Barrable and R Ponsonby Staples fantasy painting 'England v Australia at Lord's'. Amongst the gathering of famous personages of the time Lillie Langtry sits coyly avoiding the gaze of her lover, the Prince of Wales. 1958 saw its demolition to make way for the airy and spaciously impersonal two tier Warner Stand. Plum Warner's ashes were scattered on the grass in front of his stand.

Immediately behind the A Stand was a large grassy mound sloping upwards to a height of about six feet high. For the Eton v. Harrow matches several horse-drawn coaches would be hauled up to this vantage point overlooking the ground – whether the gentry actually watched the cricket over the roof of the A Stand or could be better seen watching I was never quite certain. Half a dozen or so coaches also arrayed themselves along the boundary fence on the Tavern concourse. All these vehicles arrived on the backs of lorries and we never saw a horse – no doubt in bygone times huge numbers of coaches would bring the aristocratic spectators from central London to watch the match. Late one evening my father was having a gentle stroll around the ground and happened upon a couple of villains removing cases of wine from a coach. He informed them that the police were on their way. They beat a hasty retreat into the darkness and the liquid hospitality for the second day was thankfully preserved.

Even in the 1950s a good many thousand spectators were attracted to the Eton v. Harrow match. Everyone dressed up, with the men in top hats and tails and the ladies in very elegant and colourful frocks. They promenaded

Lillie Langtry.

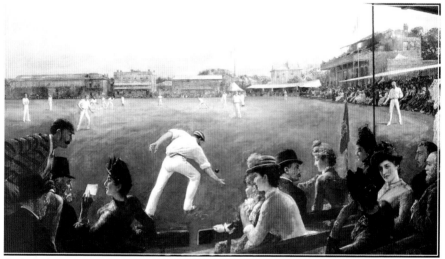

An imaginary cricket match c1880 between England and Australia by artists H Barrable and R P Staples.

The Pavilion from the Warner Stand from the same vantage point a hundred years later.

on the ground during the lunch and tea intervals and, if you weren't seen, your social standing took a catastrophic plunge. With the construction of the Warner Stand the green mound was reduced to about a third of its height and size and now supports one of the floodlight columns installed for night matches.

On the subject of seeing, I have always thought the finest view of Lord's cricket was from the scorer's box sited above the old Grand Stand scoreboard. Although side-on to the wicket, its lofty height at the top of the 'slope' and proximity to the boundary gave an almost sparrow's eye vista. Looking down on the grass and players, without the distracting background of spectators from a lower level, it was the easiest watching. Father Time had a slightly better view as he originally swivelled in the wind on the roof just above the scorer's box.

LORD'S LANDMARK

The Oval, the great south of the river rival to Lord's, is renowned for its local landmark – the somewhat unromantic gasometer. Lord's nearly competed for a while. Looking southward over the Mound Stand and old Tavern was a pre-war electricity power station. Along the banks of the Regent's Canal was a massive brick chimney a hundred and fifty feet tall at least. Adjacent were two rows of extremely ugly wooden cooling towers. They dominated the horizon.

The latter are depicted in Charles Cundall's beautiful landscape painting of England v Australia at Lord's in 1938. Curiously, the chimney, which was slightly to the left, does not feature – it may have been considered such a

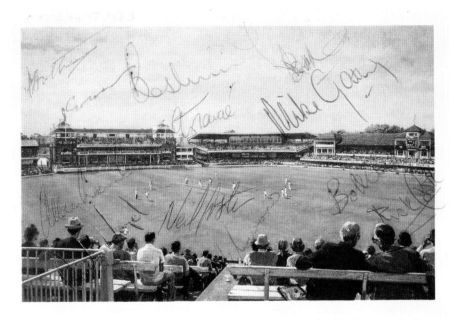

Arthur Weaver's painting of the Centenary Test Match in 1980 England v. Australia from a postcard signed by some of the players.

disfigurement to the skyline that the artist exercised his licence to exclude. It never really caught the inspiration or image of elegant Lord's. Then, in the 1960s, the coolers evaporated out of existence, soon to be followed by the chimney's disappearance, with a resultant plummet in second-hand brick prices in the north London area. It was a not very pretty but distinctive feature of the Lord's southern panorama.

My favourite Lord's picture is Arthur Weaver's England v Australia in 1980 from the back of the Free Seats looking towards the Pavilion and Warner Stand. It captures the essence of cricket watching with spectators in the foreground wearing an array of hats to keep off the sun. Some are engaged in quiet conversation but all are relaxed and contentedly absorbed in the conflict raging before them.

A view from Century Court.

Lord's Tavern in the 1950s with backdrop of the old power station in Lodge Road.

7

COLLECTING AND THE ARTS

AUTOGRAPH HUNTING

Autograph hunters were regarded by the Lord's authorities as pests and were treated accordingly. After a match, many players left the ground on foot, usually through the Grace Gates. Hopeful small boys clutching their books and pens would hang about and beg for signatures. If lucky, they might get one or two but they were quickly rounded up and ejected, dejected, by the commissionaires.

Many years later a long-standing friend confessed to me that just before play finished he and a pal used to slip into the Clock Tower bar. As it was hardly ever used they hid amongst the beer barrels under the counter for twenty minutes or so then slunk out to ambush the celebrities – he is very proud of his autograph collection.

Hopeful collectors posted in their autograph books to Lord's requesting them to be autographed by individual players or, if possible, entire teams. The signing

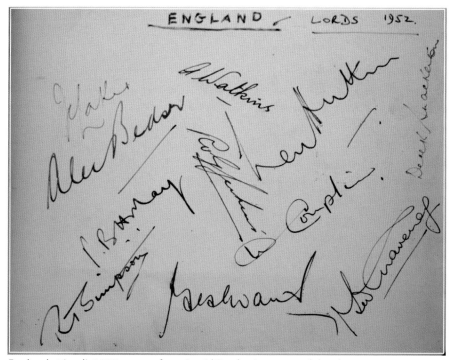

England at Lord's 1952, a page from David Dunbar's autograph book.

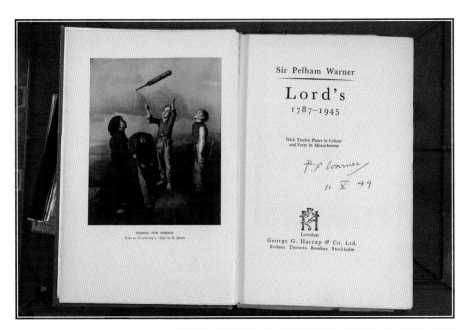

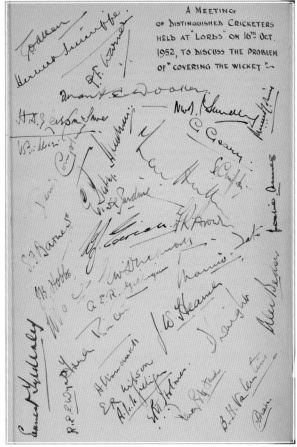

Sir Pelham Warner's Lord's which became a unique autograph book.

of autograph books was controlled by the dressing room attendants. At this point history is best left vague but, suffice to say, players signed a specimen sheet and the attendants were kept busy sending back the books to their presumably well-pleased owners.

My own autograph book spent much of its life in the tender care of the attendants who I liked to think made sure it accompanied the sample sheets for the players' signatures. After my father retired from Lord's I discovered he had a copy of Sir Pelham Warner's famous book 'Lord's, 1787–1945' which, some might say, was desecrated by being used as an autograph book for over twenty five years. 'Lord's' was genuinely signed by most of the home and visiting sides from 1949 to 1975. Many other great names of the game appear randomly amongst the text. In 1952 there was a meeting of distinguished cricketers held at Lord's to discuss 'the problem of covering the wicket'. Nearly forty worthies signed the 'Lord's' book including such famous names as Jack Hobbs, Gubby Allen, Herbert Sutcliffe, Sidney Barnes, Doug Wright, Bob Wyatt, Len Hutton, Pelham Warner and Bill Voce to mention a few. Don Bradman has signed his photograph opposite page 244!

DRESS CODE FLOUTED

There is one other notable sporting celebrity to be found on page 15. On 16 May 1966 Cassius Clay, aka Muhammad Ali, then approaching the zenith of his heavyweight boxing career, visited Lord's during a West Indian Test Match. His autograph was in a then steady and firm hand. Sitting with Gary Sobers in the West Indian dressing room Ali was disdainfully uninterested in cricket watching. Judging by his appearance it seems no one, perhaps wisely, had ventured to suggest he comply with the Pavilion dress code by wearing a jacket and tie. At least my father had the courage to ask him for his autograph.

Jim Dunbar's cryptic comment next to the signature of Muhammad Ali.

TOP: *Muhammad Ali joins Gary Sobers in the West Indian dressing room.*

RIGHT: *Muhammad Ali displays his batting skills – largely unknown until this moment.*

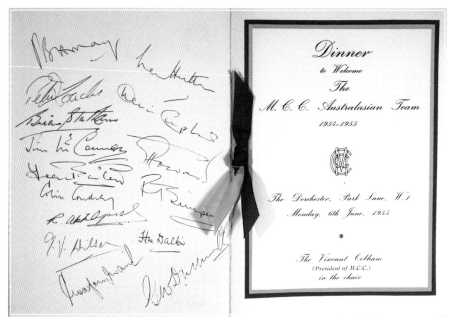

A typical MCC Dinner menu from the 1950s.

DINNERS AND MENUS

Among the more discreet social activities of Lord's life were the dinners held in the Pavilion or the Tavern, formerly in the old restaurant and in recent years in the new building's Thomas Lord Suite. Occasionally they strayed down Park Lane to the Dorchester Hotel. The Annual Members' Dinner and the dinner for the visiting touring team were the main events with one-offs for retirements, anniversaries and the like. In the 1950s it was customary to circulate the menu cards which all or most of those present would sign. Such mementos are a unique record of those of the cricket elite who wined and dined at the heart of the game. A good price for signed menus is usually forthcoming on eBay. The fare, for those days, was grand; 'consommé, chicken wings with peas and new potatoes, fruit salad and ice cream' and a savoury washed down with coffee. In recent decades the signing of menu cards seems to have gradually faded in popularity, but father still kept on menu autograph hunting for forty years and ended up with an historic collection. Some sporting memorabilia, especially in football and boxing, has become big business but beware of forgers and fakers.

MEMORIAL GALLERY AND MUSEUM

The Lord's Memorial Gallery or Museum is the focal point for cricket art and artefacts. When we arrived at Lord's there was no museum – only a rather leaky racquets court and two squash courts. Squash Court B was the worst with slippery puddles draining from the roof at the slightest suggestion of rain.

The racquets court was gutted and the shell converted into the fine Memorial Gallery and finished in 1953. It was dedicated to cricketers who lost their lives in the two World Wars.

The cricket associated art consists of an unrivalled collection of paintings, prints, books, silverware, trophies, ceramics and general cricketing bric-a-brac with records going back well over two hundred years. Artefacts come as an array of motley clothing and bats, balls, stumps, equipment and anything you can think of to do with the game. Recently there has been a surging interest in what has become known as cricketana, much of which has accumulated at Lord's. A stroll round the gallery invariably enthuses even those cynical few

The newly finished Memorial Gallery and Museum. The Ashes often resided on the window sill to the left.

The Ashes somehow managed to find their way into our backgarden to be photographed with a half pint beer bottle to illustrate their diminutive scale.

who resolutely insist on being bored by cricket: the sparrow killed by a cricket ball in 1936 and the Ashes under a glass dome had a new home on the window sill on the first floor. Anyone could sneak along and slip the Ashes, only 11cm high, into a pocket – no CCTV security in those days.

In fact, there was some concern that this might come to pass. Being so small, only a few inches tall, the Ashes could very easily go walkabout or get lost, rather like the competition they symbolise. I was once told of consternation within the inner circles of the MCC organisation that the Ashes urn displayed was, in fact, just a replica (of which there were several). The original was usually stuck away for safe keeping somewhere in the bowels of the Pavilion. Then the original and replicas were moved around and got muddled up – and no-one could really tell the difference. Subsequently, I never heard that the problem was actually resolved.

After World War II the MCC library and cricket collection were curated by Diana Rait Kerr. She was stationed in what is now the Old Library, the room at the top of the main Pavilion entrance stairs on the left. Here the books and records were housed, with the paintings and prints hung in the Long Room and scattered around the Pavilion. The surplus stock remained in the basement out of sight but with periodic clear-outs to make way for exhibits displaced by donated or purchased new material which had to be shown. Little monetary value was attached to cricket related items so unwanted or damaged stock was often thrown out or given away. 'I've had a clear-out, does anyone want this stuff'. Diana offered prints, photos and redundant exhibits and so they went to staff or anyone who happened to be around.

Diana Rait Kerr, the first Lord's curator of the library and museum from 1946 to 1968. Here she is on cricket watching tour on her way home from Australia.

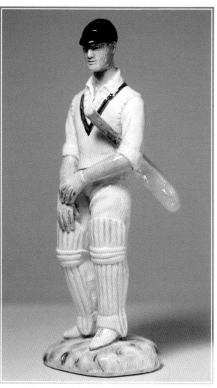

A figurine by Mary Mitchell- Smith.

The executive hierarchy at Lord's generally was fairly oblivious of artistic merit or the impending popularity and increasing value of what became known by collectors and auction houses as 'cricketana'. When Billy Griffith departed his job as Secretary of Sussex County Cricket club to take up his appointment as an Assistant Secretary of MCC he was presented with a leaving present. This was a fine old engraving from a painting by William Drummond of the famous cricket match played between Sussex and Kent at Brighton, published in 1849. Of considerable artistic and historical interest there is more than one version of this view with the church and sea beyond. The print was relegated to an out-building of his home where it languished for many years. When the subsequent occupants also moved home the minor treasure was abandoned but, fortunately, being well framed and glazed it survived the damp and neglect to be finally rescued.

My father, however, did have a good eye for art and early on at Lord's Mary Mitchell-Smith, a local sculptor, had produced a fine ceramic figure of a batsman which was presented to the museum. As she lived locally in Grove End Gardens she commissioned another version but painted with the colours of the Butterflies CC and dated 1953. The relaxed position of the batsman padded up, bat under arm and putting on his gloves about to go in to bat captures an evocative aspect of the contemporary game.

Stephen Green, Lord's museum curator from 1968 to 2003, took the view that the relentlessly inflating values of cricket art and collectables have had a detrimental effect on the museum's ability to purchase exhibits. The art market fuelled by the wealth of private collectors often precludes the acquisition of important items of artistic or historical interest for display to a wider public audience.

The Christies' 1987 Bicentenary Auction catalogue.

The impending market explosion was not anticipated but gradually began to be realised in the 1960s with enthusiastic and increasingly affluent collectors splashing out their money. This culminated at Christie's MCC Bicentenary Auction of MCC cast-offs and duplicates in 1987 when rich collectors were separated from a substantial portion of their wealth.

The catalogue was a mouth-watering and unrepeated selection of over eight hundred lots which bidders fought over tooth and nail. Paintings, prints, photographs, books, clothing, ceramics, ephemera and clutter were indiscriminately snapped up. The day-long sale took place in the Tavern banqueting room and an adjoining annexe with television screens so bids could be waved to a second rostrum. Both rooms were packed solid with members, dealers and the public, all anxious for a piece of the action. I had an eye on several lots but prices were astronomically over the estimates and, if there were any bargains, it may have been much later in the afternoon, and all for the second-rate stuff that Lord's was just discarding. The Lord's sale helped to amass a fund in excess of £300k for additions to the Lord's treasure trove of cricket art and memorabilia.

As result of this new-found affluence MCC has been is a position in the last decade to commission many new works of art – mostly paintings of grounds or even particularly important matches as well as portraits of players. The infinite variety of styles by modern artists would leave the traditional painters of the eighteenth and nineteenth centuries aghast at what they might now see. The modern-day 'Conversation Piece' portrays a group of famous cricketing personalities watching a game through the window of the Committee Room. Hence the Victorian manner of recognising the good and the great for posterity is achieved in just one work. That said, the portrait of Shane Warne tossing a ball and gazing threateningly the length of the Long Room has dramatic impact. Depicting cricket matches has never been easy and recent paintings, whilst bright and sunny, rarely capture the atmosphere or intimacy of the game and spectators. The latter in the foreground, if well composed, are very likely to please the eye by enhancing the landscape.

WISDEN ON OFFER

On one occasion the Secretariat was opening the usual morning post to find a letter from a widow wanting to sell her late husband's complete run of Wisdens. 'We don't want them – Jim, you answer her.' He did and soon became the proud owner of a complete set of John Wisden Cricketers' Almanacks starting in 1864. All the early volumes were uniformly rebound and complete with a photograph or picture as the frontispiece, so often missing in odd volumes which come up for sale. The next section was in a red cloth binding and the rest in the brown cloth hard back. All in all it was a fine set for which father paid a very fair price for the time but he had little idea as to how quickly the value would inflate dramatically. After he retired the Wisdens were not consulted much but it was still with some sadness we eventually decided to sell the set in the hope that a keen cricketer might enjoy them.

A set of Guyanan stamps.

Since childhood my father had been an enthusiastic stamp collector and, after his retirement in 1978, he concentrated on assembling a thematic cricket collection. He travelled far and wide to seek out any stamp which featured cricket in some way, however obvious or obscure the association might be. The collection was close to definitive which, after his death in 1987, I maintained up to the year 2000. A few years later MCC generously purchased the collection and my father would be very pleased that his stamps now reside in the museum at Lord's.

PHOTOGRAPHS

This brings me to my father's photography. At a time in the 1950s when colour photography was yet to become universal and, indeed, still a rarity in cricketing circles, he was in a unique situation. As a keen photographer, he was given permission to take photographs in Lord's where all other rights were held by agency, but they only did black and white pictures for the newspapers. He had a succession of old Leica cameras which had superb glass in the lenses, thus producing pin-sharp images and excellent colour rendition. Even restricted to a standard 50mm lens and view finder he achieved results which could not be improved on today.

In Jim Swanton's book, the dustjacket and frontispiece have a close-up view of Father Time set against a clear blue sky but slightly spoiled by a long streak of pigeon poo. Dad had climbed through a filthy dusty trap door to a thoroughly precarious perch on the roof of the Grand Stand to get the picture. He had expected me, as his assistant, to do the same but at least I was not expected to scrub down the old man with the scythe. The incredible bird's eye view of the ground was not one many people have risked their lives to see.

For the best part of twenty years his Father Time picture, along with many other photos, was used by MCC for postcards sold at the ground and they are a good colour record of Lord's in the 1950s and '60s. Although never paid a penny or the price of a film, Dad was just happy to see them being useful. He concentrated on crowd scenes and, around the ground, the quirky or unusual which the press people tended to ignore. Sadly, early Kodachrome transparencies were not always colourfast and I am now the proud owner of several drawers full of blank slides – a tantalising loss. But at least the later pictures from the early 1960s have survived well and help to bring these reminiscences alive.

The first colour view of Lord's from the newly built Lord's View flats.

While watching the 1963 West Indies Test Match I remember a sudden look of absolute horror on my mother's face. There, a good one hundred and fifty feet up, perched on the unguarded roof of the nearly completed block of flats, was the figure of my father clutching his camera minutely silhouetted against the skyline. Appropriately named Lord's View (Phase One), this is what he had clambered up to get for the first time.

Since it was a Saturday, the site was empty of workmen but the gates had been left open; no Health and Safety in those days, fortunately. As the roof of the Mound Stand was then lower, virtually the whole ground was visible and he snapped one of the best views ever taken of Lord's and with a full house. I have searched the photo carefully to spot my mother and me who were sitting opposite in the Grand Stand.

Once the single lens reflex camera took over, the professionals, such as Patrick Eagar, moved in to dominate the photographic scene. Sophisticated gear meant long-distance and action shots in colour were routine. Colour printing has developed in the last decade, enabling stunning images to be routine. MCC now has a Design and Printing department producing high quality material including newsletters, brochures, catalogues and literature for members and the public to a standard unimaginable in the past.

8

MEDIA ENTERTAINMENT

THE PRESS

We encountered many well-known journalists and broadcasters. The press used to call us at all times of the day and night, especially if there was some cricket crisis or scandal on the brew. It was my job to answer the 'phone if there was the slightest suspicion Dad was to be quizzed for an inside story. At the age of seven I had a script along the line that I would go and 'ask my Dad if he was in' – gradually I developed more sophisticated responses as protection from the prying vultures. Our 'phone number was Cunningham 9689. For a few years a new exchange was named Lord's but that soon went when only numbers could be dialled.

From a very young age my cynicism for the press was nourished by an inside knowledge of the true facts. I remember a long article about some cricket story my father was closely involved with. The writer managed to perpetrate at least one factual error in every single short paragraph throughout the article. Some were blindingly obvious; others blatantly over-sexed the story or were inconsistent with other inaccuracies. Every minor event was exaggerated or misconstrued into 'a crisis'. Yet an unscrupulous national newspaper encouraged some shameless journalist to concoct utter drivel and lies to mislead their readers. This fetid behaviour seems to be a necessity to sell newspapers and has yet to be reversed. An invaluable lesson for life: never believe what you read in the press. There were, however, exceptions that one had to learn to recognise and respect.

GOOD AND LESS GOD

The Johnston family lived in Cavendish Avenue, a few yards from the North Gate, so Brian was often seen at Lord's – at least we had that in common. In contrast to some other journalists he was an unfailingly friendly man who always said 'Hello, David' and asked a question proving that he remembered exactly what he had talked about to this small boy last time. 'How are the leg breaks?' or 'What are you playing on the guitar now?' Even if he was in hurry there was always a good chat.

Many well-deserved tributes have been paid to Brian. I happened to be on a family holiday in Swanage when we met his widow, Pauline, who invited us

The memorial plaque to Brian Johnston in the park behind St John's Wood church. Lord's can be seen through the trees with the Media Centre dominating the horizon.

Brian Johnston interviewing Peter May.

A news vendor's hoarding exhorting Telegraph readers to 'Read E.W. Swanton'!

to visit his newly erected gravestone in the cemetery looking high over the English Channel. A while later a tulip tree was planted in Brian's memory in the church burial ground adjoining Wellington Road opposite Lord's – it is growing well and Brian would be amused by the irony of a humour-free Council which placed a municipal plaque, next to his commemoration, with the edict 'No Ball Games'. He would have had a good chuckle but more recently the sign has disappeared. The Brian Johnston film theatre in the museum was donated by John P Getty in 1994.

Len Hutton and David at home in 1953 photographed by Jim Dunbar who never missed a photo op.

In stark contrast was the revered Daily Telegraph correspondent, writer and broadcaster E W Swanton, known to his friends as Jim, although few knew what the E W stood for. We had been introduced on several occasions. Either he had a very poor memory for faces, was shy or did not acknowledge the existence of less important mortals than himself. We frequently passed by in Lord's but without a glimmer of recognition or conversation.

Swanton's great godly opus, The World of Cricket, first published in 1966, was embellished with many colour photographs mostly taken by my father at a time when colour photography was not widespread and a rarity in cricket. Some are classic cricket views. Swanton said he 'wasn't going to make money out of the book', which was hard to believe. Certainly some gesture of royalties is still awaited … but my father was happy that many of his best early photos were preserved for posterity and accompanied by such a fine text.

Douglas Glass, the New Zealand photographer, made his name with A Weekly Portrait Gallery of famous people in The Sunday Times. In the summer of 1953 he chose as his studio the seclusion of our back garden to take Len Hutton in full batting gear. The portrait with a brief biography must have appeared in the newspaper a week or so later. My father never missed a photo chance and snapped me with the great English batsman when the serious business was finished.

'IN TOWN TONIGHT' UNDER THE TRAIN

This Saturday night radio programme was almost compulsory listening in the 1950s. One of the regular features involved Audrey Russell commentating from some well-known place or landmark with a description of where she was broadcasting from but not saying where it was. The listeners had to guess the location which was announced at the end of the half hour. It was a very dark winter's evening when my father accompanied her to the scorer's box at the top of the Grand Stand. With Father Time creaking in the wind just above, it would have been cold and gloomy if not thoroughly spooky up there. Going out live, he managed to deliver an intriguing account of the stand's history from handwritten notes lit by a flickering torch. Not many people would have had a clue where they were.

In Town Tonight was the same programme in which Brian Johnston lay on the railway sleepers between the rails of the Thames Victoria Bridge and broadcast while the London to Brighton train thundered over him. What price the health and safety killjoys allowing that now?

Amusing the players during non-playing interludes was a matter which was not really on the Lord's agenda. However, although my father did not have direct responsibility for cricket administration, he had some charge of running facilities such as the players' changing and dining rooms which meant that he had close contact with all teams hosted at Lord's. Casting back, the first eight years of his life had been spent in India where his father worked as a government civil engineer. Having been brought up by ayahs, he spoke very little English until he was sent home to boarding school. He could, however, remember many of the usual nursery rhymes, such as Humpty Dumpty, Jack and Jill and the like which he had been taught in Hindustani. Indian touring teams were treated to recitals which were unique entertainment, particularly when rain stopped play. No other MCC official was known to possess such unexpected, albeit limited, linguistic talent.

9

RANDOM TALES (Best not Told)

ROYAL INTRODUCTION

Prince Philip was due to meet a visiting Australian team before their tour started. All the meticulous arrangements were made and a call from Buckingham Palace warned Lord's that he had left and would arrive in a few minutes. In those days he drove himself in, I think, an MG. Nearly half an hour later the long line of cricketers togged in their new immaculately creaseless blazers arrayed in front of the Tavern were getting distinctly fidgety – and no sign of any Royalty, but everyone one was looking in the wrong direction. He had come in by the North Gate, not the Grace Gates, found the far end of the line and begun introducing himself as it were backwards. The welcome party of high level officials and captains were wondering if he had been kidnapped, had a prang or even gone to the Oval. Almost too late they realised their reception job was really not necessary.

NAUGHTY BOYS

Gaining admittance into Lord's for a Test Match was a challenge. Finding a seat in the free seats was a tussle for the early birds requiring enthusiasm and dedication. Queuing all night was the option, but boring and uncomfortable. Nocturnal attempts at scaling perimeter walls were not unheard of. Even in some obscure back-street of St John's Wood it was a forlorn chance as the authorities were unsportingly aware of the weaker points round the ground. In fact, breaking into Lord's was no easier than breaking out of Colditz.

For a small band of youthful bravadoes the solution was – ice cream. It did offer a near foolproof means of evading the security. An acquaintance of mine had a girlfriend whose family connections with the Wall's Ice Cream empire enabled him and a couple of pals to achieve free entrance for a day's cricket watching whenever they wanted. Soon after dawn at a rendezvous two blocks away from the ground, a deep refrigerated Wall's van would halt briefly by the traffic lights – just long enough for them to hop into the back. They had a risky few minutes to survive without frost-bite or a solidly frozen fate amongst stacks of huge crates of ice cream. Wearing winter coats and gloves might have aroused suspicions in mid-summer. They were then whisked through the Grace Gates into the ground, backed up to one of the Wall's blue and yellow kiosks and delivered discreetly and unobserved along with the day's supply of ice creams and lollies. As they arrived before the public were admitted a choice of the best unreserved seats awaited their pleasure.

SPRINGING A LEAK

One night, at about one o'clock, we were woken by frantic banging on our back door. A very agitated night watchman reported that the newly built Warner Stand was 'flooded'. Up we all got to investigate. Clad in pyjamas and wellies, my father and I discovered water gushing out of a conduit in the basement – with a massive electricity cable steaming like a kettle. A main had burst somewhere in St John's Wood or further afield as other floods were later reported.

Soon four fire engines arrived. The fireman took one look at the six foot deep water in the cellar and live electricity cables and beat a very hasty retreat shouting, 'Get out, it'll go up!' (And we'll be sunk without trace.) Water mains all over north-west London were turned off and eventually they found the culprit. Though not before waves from the extensive basement area were lapping the top of the stairs.

Pumps from two engines created a spectacular torrent of water rushing down the sloping roadway under the arches at the back of the Pavilion. Luckily, in those days there was a curb on either side preventing thousands of gallons flooding through the Pavilion entrance. Down past Q Stand it tsunamied and through the Grace Gates into an inundated St John's Wood Road – the Warner Stand was saved.

DOUBLE DE-CLUTCH

At the age of about thirteen I first learnt to drive in Lord's. A convenient mini-Monaco circuit wound under the Grand Stand, across the Nursery Ground car park, back behind the Mound Stand, in front of the Tavern concourse and home through the arches behind the Pavilion. On Sunday afternoons my father installed me in his short wheel-base Land Rover and round the ground we went – never in higher than second gear. The vehicle was a nightmare to drive but honed my ability to double de-clutch and handle the very weighty steering. The fabric of the Ground just survived and eventually I passed the test some years later.

THE BIG MACK

In many ways life was relatively relaxed in those days. For example, Dad had a Lord's master key that opened practically everything – the Pavilion entrance doors, the tennis and squash courts, the small wicket gates in each ground gate (North, East and West) and the side door by the Grace Gates. My mother also had a master key, and as a teenager so did I – we could go anywhere in Lord's – what a dream but in fact I took it entirely for granted and perfectly normal. A night watchman once lost a complete set of keys, including a master; Dad was not pleased but nobody else seemed too bothered and certainly no locks were ever changed.

Security at Lord's was questionably high, or was it low, on the agenda as far as the Ticket Office staff were concerned. At the end of each day's play the gate takings were gathered and counted in the Pavilion, often late into the evening. Just cash – no credit cards in those days. The story was, and I remember seeing them often, Charlie Wray, the boss, and Audrey Jones, his assistant and bodyguard, would then make their way, via the North Gate, to the night deposit safe of the St John's Wood branch of Barclays Bank.

Charlie carried a large, rather ostentatious but battered leather decoy briefcase and Audrey, nothing. He always donned a long shabby macintosh whatever the weather, even in high summer. Apparently this was the forerunner of the shoplifter's outfit with huge inside pockets in which vast

Charlie Wray at his retirement party. Assistant Secretary, Ronnie Ford, is in the background

bundles of notes, the day's cash takings, were stuffed. They always took the same route. Over the years the money arrived without fail at the bank and they went off home safely. How the coins got to the bank was a closely kept secret.

MONKEY BUSINESS

Occasionally the Nursery End car park played overnight host to the owner of some famous chimpanzees which he brought to London in his campervan. Although London Zoo was just along the road they needed a more discreet place for the night and where better than off-season Lord's. They had not come to watch cricket. These highly trained, but mischievous, uncontrollable chimps, starred in the PG Tips TV advertisements. They were filmed somewhere in the West End and were good fun to visit before they returned home somewhere up North. Only my father, the gateman and one or two people in the know ever saw the apes. They all wore nappies which were laundered and hung on a line by the North Gate.

Celebrity apes hang their nappies out to dry under the North Gate arbours.

The PG Tips chimps behind the perspex window of their camper van.

DARLING

The 1965 British film drama starred Julie Christie, Laurence Harvey and Dirk Bogarde. A year before, Lord's was taken over for four days as a set for shooting several scenes. There was plenty of standing around although Christie smouldered in her own deckchair. Unusually for Lord's, heavy artificial rain had to halt play thanks to two hoses which drowned extras in the Warner Stand. Disappointingly the sequences never appeared in the film!

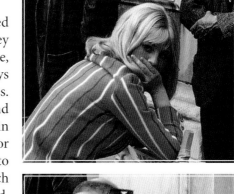

PIGEON PIE

Other dangers lurked around the ground. The head groundsman from 1936 to 1955 was Austin Martin who resided in a pleasant grace and favour cottage located by the East Gate, (long since demolished to make way for the Lord's shop). On Sunday mornings he patrolled Lord's with a twelve bore shotgun. His hatred of the pigeons, which devoured precious grass seed lovingly sown to repair the hallowed square, was legendary. However, he began to stray from potting the pigeons on the pitch and to blasting these tiresome pests off the gutters and roof of the Pavilion and other stands. Destroying the pavilion by gunfire was a step too far and had to be stopped. We never discovered what he had for his Sunday roast lunch after that. Apparently he moved on from Lord's to manage a pub in Surrey.

A GREAT FLAPPING BATSMAN

Peter May became a close family friend and had several holidays with us boating on the Thames. His home town was Reading so we moored our cabin cruiser by the bridge where we rendezvoused and he clambered on board to become a junior crew member. In those days the cricket season fizzled out in early September so he had time for a break. After one particularly successful summer he was recognised by the lock keeper at Nuneham just upstream from Oxford. He telephoned his mate at the next lock and for the rest of the day there was an assortment of welcoming parties at each successive lock. Being late summer and in the country there were usually wasps buzzing around. I recall him furiously flapping them away. Fast bowlers held no terrors for him but he was terrified of wasps. Peter did much to encourage my cricketing enthusiasm and even found time on overseas tours with MCC to send me postcards and letters.

Batsmen in the twenty-first century are relatively well protected from fast bowling. One has to admire the bravery of the earlier batsmen, who had to stand up to ferociously fast and intimidating bowlers, without helmets, thigh and chest pads, arm guards and the like. Often batsmen in the 1950s came in to bat bare-headed not even with a cap. Peter May was no exception. The likes of Ray Lindwall, Keith Miller, Fred Trueman, and Frank Tyson were all major proponents of battering the opposition back to the pavilion, although there was an occasional unwritten truce between late order bowlers not to bowl too aggressively at each other.

By the Thames, Peter May advises David on the finer points of angling. Peter caught much more in the slips.

THE NUN'S STORY

One of my father's duties was to sort out problems facing the Secretariat and there was no escape when these problems arrived at the morning post opening. One instance was a letter from a nun in France announcing that she was coming to England the following week with a coach load of her teenage school pupils. They were very dedicated to learning about 'the English way of life and what better place to come than Lord's to watch cricket being played'!

The letter's charming but insistent tone had the aura of a command from On High. Needless to say my father was delegated to act as host and he instantly co-opted my mother who spoke a little French. I was also roped in. The group consisted of some forty girls and their inspirational teacher Soeur Lazare and several novices to keep order. Their visitation was extremely polite and appeared to be a great success but what they really thought we shall never know. In the event they returned for several years. Sister Lazare was formidable and we all became firm friends. She prayed for us 'every day'. We were invited to visit her convent in Normandy and were regally entertained with fine wines at dinner and a night in a convent. Life at Lord's opened many doors!

WG Grace is crowned King of France.

10

ST JOHN'S WOOD

'THE WOOD'

It has to be remembered that the legacy of wartime was still strong in everyone's memory and starkly evident realities even in leafy green St John's Wood. So soon after the Second World War, Lord's was inevitably run-down, a bit shabby and dilapidated. In the 1950s the spectators' walk from St John's Wood tube station to Lord's was a somewhat desolate spectacle. That said, the station entrance had delightful well-tended flower beds and sub-tropical trees to greet the crowds on their way to Lord's. I believe it won prizes for the best kept station but that was a long time ago – now it is a scruffy neglected mess. Maybe Lord's might sponsor the upkeep of the entrance gardens in exchange for a little local advertising and publicity for cricket.

Bombs had fallen all around in St John's Wood but luckily the ground had escaped any serious damage. The entire block opposite the station by the Circus Road bus stop was an ugly hole in the ground. Now it is occupied by the Post Office, library and council flats. Wellington Road was a motley collection of scruffy buildings now replaced by blocks of luxury flats and hospitals. The current BP garage and flats were an open forecourt where one had a choice of half a dozen different brands of petrol, all at more or less the same price. There was no such thing as self-service so one had to wait for the attendant to fill up the tank. Behind the pumps was a long line of single storey lock-ups, all mostly derelict. Abandoned Victorian houses lay empty and decaying along St John's Wood Road, eventually to be replaced by Lord's View and other blocks of flats overlooking Lord's.

A walk from our house across the north side of Lord's was a short cut to the St John's Wood shops in the High Street or the church by the roundabout. 'The Wood', as it was affectionately referred to by long-standing residents, was a village with high street shops where you could buy anything from the family businesses and many of the inhabitants had lived there all their lives. Butchers, bakers, grocers, open-slab fishmonger, chemists, hardware and the like all thrived in the 1950s. Family businesses abounded. The Bent family had a drapery shop in Circus Road with a toy section deep in the rear where they probably lost more than they sold according to a school friend who knew the place intimately. Mr Brown's grocery store in St John's Wood Terrace opposite The Star pub offered same day delivery. The communal spirit was, nonetheless, poised to move towards extinction.

The Roundabout by Lord's. Passed by most visitors to Lord's with the statue of St George and the dragon in the foreground.

St John's Wood church celebrated the bi-centenary of its consecration in1814, the same year Lord's settled on the present site just across Wellington Road.

St John's Wood Adventure Playground. The 1972 Australian team show local kids a straight bat. Left to right, Brian Taber, Bruce Francis and Rod Marsh (his first tour to England).

Most of the original pubs thrived but gradually closed or degenerated into impersonal chain restaurants; the Portland Arms (Carluccios), the Sir Isaac Newton (Café Rouge), the Princess Royal (Sofra, then Fora), the Red House, the Knights of St John, The Heroes of Alma, the Rose and Crown (subsequently the Rossetti, but now flats), and the original Lord's Tavern will all be held in distant affection by the lunchtime and after play drinkers.

Now the High Street is a mecca for very expensive clothes boutiques, equally over-priced cafés and restaurants which are frequented by tinted window cars often double parked by owners who do not walk anywhere and certainly would find the cricket over the road incomprehensible. Two separate worlds living next to each other. The soul of 'The Wood' is, I hope, guarded by the statue of St John the Baptist in the church yard at the southern end of the High Street.

BEATLE BLOCK – ELM TREE ROAD

This quiet little L-shaped road where we lived in the heart of St John's Wood just north of Lord's had a leafy charm with an almost rural ambience. A massive elm tree grew at the Circus Road end, forcing a gap in the old brick wall until

Whilst nostalgically missed, the original Lord's Tavern was replaced by a modern building fifty yards along St John's Wood Road with expanded pub and dining facilities. Regrettably it did not offer a view of the ground or cricket.

One of the oldest known pillar boxes – opposite the North Gate.

the Dutch disease finally had its way. Opposite our house was a single storey cottage, reputedly the original farm house, with a yard at the side. The buildings behind were stables and I was told rings in the walls were for tethering the cows at milking time. By the 1950s the romance had evaporated as it was used an overflow storage garage for Hamilton Motors who sold cars in the Edgware Road.

The southern side of Elm Tree Road, with ten houses, was owned by MCC and backed onto Lord's. The other side of the block was Cavendish Avenue where Beatle, Paul McCartney, had his London residence and from where in the 1960s he walked his Old English sheepdog in Regent's Park. Living on the same block as a Beatle was considered prestigious in some circles, particularly of those who did not understand the importance of cricket. The Beatles made most of their records at the EMI recording studios which were about three minutes walk from the end of our road. Outside, the zebra crossing, iconically featured on the album cover of Abbey Road, still attracts dozens of tourists every day – from all over the world, especially the Far East.

Other eminent neighbours included members of the Astor family, Max Jaffa, the musician, Emmie Tillett of the concert agents Ibbs & Tillett and a discreet band of well-to-do people. Our neighbour over the road was Jim Flitcroft, a dentist, who bought his site for £2000 and spent the same amount again building himself a nice four bedroom house. He was very proud of the roof which, unusually, was of copper sheeting that soon matured into a bright verdigris. The MP Sir Richard Pilkington, of the glass empire fame, lived with his family in Grove End Road and their back garden adjoined the side of ours. He had two daughters about my age and my father pestered me to 'do something about it'. But I was very shy in the days of my youth!

Our rubbish was collected every day and the dustman even returned the bins to our yard with the lids replaced – that was courtesy of the old St Marylebone Borough Council. The post was delivered three times a day and letters collected from the ancient pillar box on the corner of Elm Tree Road every day, including weekends. Milk was delivered daily and left in a little cubby hole in the garden wall. It was never stolen. Sam, our local cockney greengrocer, parked his truck in Scott Ellis Gardens and called at the back door on Tuesday lunchtimes for my mother's order. One of his minions, a delightful Polish refugee, delivered a box in early evening, the contents of which rarely coincided with what my mother had asked for. The fruit and veg were usually fresh but, if not, my mother did not like complaining as Sam would send round an embarrassing amount of extra stuff. Newspapers were delivered free of charge as was the meat for our Sunday lunch. Those were the days.

I remember with fury the day on which the Council painted yellow lines in the road to control parking. This seemed like an intrusion and desecration of a peaceful backwater where local kids played cricket safely in the street, and the illusion of an unpressured life began to disintegrate. That was the moment when the dead hand of authority, especially the planners, began its subservience to the greedy modern day world of property speculation and profit. Over the years the pressures for more and more expensive homes have led to the over-development of Elm Tree Road and ridiculously cramped dwellings – suffice to say there is now a block of flats in our back garden and my net and the beautiful garden of number six have also been obliterated by another ill-placed block.

BUTTERFLIES AND SPARROWS

The Colonel's wife, Mrs Rait Kerr, such was the formality in those days we never reached first name acquaintance, was a kindly but formidable character. She was a keen and very knowledgeable ornithologist so Lord's may not have been her first choice for a birder's habitat. For reasons I have never really ascertained, I developed an early and life-long fascination with butterflies and moths – a lepidopterist – so we shared a love for nature which she was always keen to talk about.

Lord's and its environs has never been much of a wildlife haven but I did once catch a Silver-washed Fritillary butterfly in the garden, quite a rarity on the edge of inner London. Being about eight at the time, I was very excited, and the unfortunate creature ended up as a short-lived exhibit in the Insect House at the London Zoo. Cabbage Whites, or Small Whites to the initiated, or *Pieris rapae* to the impressively well-informed, were always plentiful and one sunny day I remember sitting in the garden for an hour just counting as they fluttered by. There were never fewer than three and the most at any one time was eight. Small Tortoiseshells occasionally passed by but not so often. Buddleias had yet to take over as the universal wasteland weed or cultivated butterfly nectar hostelry, but toward the end of our time at Elm Tree Road a couple did seed themselves at the end of the garden.

In the twenty-first century the best place for butterfly watching in St John's Wood is along the north bank of the Regent's Park Canal west of the London Zoo. In particular the Orange Tip, Green-veined White and Brimstone are common. The Park itself now has a few more wilder patches of uncut grass on the edges of the sports fields. Several species of butterfly are well-established including the Meadow Brown and Small Skipper, thanks to some enlightened land management by the Park authorities.

Lord's has a touch of the rural even close to central London. It has managed to preserve a few mature trees here and there, most notably the plane trees behind the Compton

Silver-washed Fritillary, a rare visitor near the centre of London.

and Edrich stands, the greenery of which softens the hard architecture of the stands and is visible to most spectators. Behind the Warner Stand and around the Coronation Garden the trees have been well preserved. Squirrels now seem more plentiful and tame. A line of lime trees drip stickily on to the elite committee parking spaces and several horse-chestnuts have always produced their fine harvest of conkers. In the autumn I became very popular with friends who knew of my exclusive untouched harvest of conkers which was a priceless currency on the school playground commodity market. We collected hundreds of Lord's conkers every year.

Watching the cricket from the open stands, one was never alone, especially during matches seriously bereft of spectators. The ubiquity of sparrows was taken for granted – twittering and hopping around the benches and under our feet in search of and squabbling over sandwich crumbs. They were plentiful in the time of the Colonel's wife but now they are a rarity – I am sure she would be horrified at their rapid decline in more recent years. Herds of fat London wood pigeons used to waddle across the ground but I have the impression they are far less common than during the immediate post-war era. Even the seagulls seem to shun Lord's and find better foraging in Regent's Park or amongst the rubbish down the road in the Church Street market. Gastronomically speaking, the grass is possibly more of a desert now, being rolled harder and trimmed shorter. I doubt if there are many resident worms at Lord's nowadays.

The only other animal life around the Ground, albeit temporary, were the police horses which patrolled the streets to control big match crowds.

11

NEW ERAS

NUMBER 11 TO 1

During his playing career Dad invariably found himself at the bottom of the batting order at number 11. Even when captaining a side he seemed happy to do this, although it did not reflect his ability to score runs. Off the field of play he coped with almost any administrative duty and, indeed, chores at Lord's other than the cricket itself. He was the Secretarial number 11 and often the senior longstop, so he said. As an example, years later I found his notes for a speech to 350 members at The Cricket Society Annual Dinner in 1969 which he had only a few hours to prepare – in place of Maurice Allom, an MCC Committee member, who was unexpectedly immobilised by gout. He also presented John Barclay with The Most Promising Cricketer of the Year Award. Other speakers were Rachel Heyhoe and Ronald Mason who complimented father by saying he was one of the only two people at Lord's 'who could read and write'.

Jim Dunbar at Lord's in 1980 after his retirement.

The same year saw a significant change of fortune and a new career. Cricket in Britain was undergoing radical reorganisation and MCC was about to relinquish control of cricket. Democratisation was the name of the game; the Test and County Board was created and the National Cricket Association, NCA, formed to nurture amateur cricket including club, services and schools cricket, coaching, artificial pitches and the Village competition. MCC kept guardianship of the Rules but not much else. Father thought this was 'selling its birthright on the off-chance that the Government

119

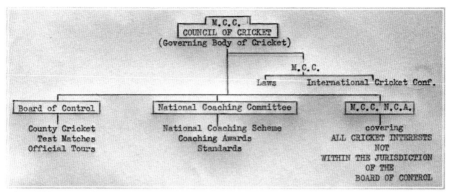

The old hierachy for the administration of cricket.

might give cricket some money'. None of us foresaw what Sky would do for cricket.

Luckily, nobody was made redundant. A personnel reshuffle was instigated and father was appointed the first Secretary of NCA under a new committee chaired by Freddie Brown, a former England captain. MCC still paid his salary and he stayed in the same office in the Pavilion until his retirement in 1978. The new job was a fresh breath of life and gave him much greater freedom whilst still remaining in the heart of Lord's. He believed strongly in the importance and value of installing artificial wickets for clubs and schools as practice nets and, where suitable, for match wickets. His expertise led him to a close relationship with Dunlop and other companies producing long-lasting and low maintenance cricket surfaces.

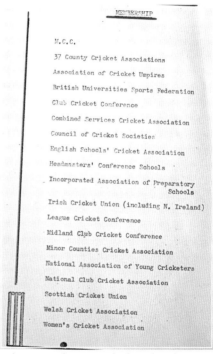

The original papers which outlined NCA's responsibilities from the orginal file.

RETIREMENT

Approaching the time of his retirement MCC decided that the house at Elm Tree Road was destined for disposal to raise money for further ground redevelopment. My parents then settled in a flat in Westbourne Grove which was a ten minute drive from Lord's and an easy commute. The cogs turned painfully slowly and our house was left empty for a while but soon put to good use by the local squatters before being sold several years later – a sad end to an era of unique living. Now there is a block of flats in our garden and another straddling the net area and into the next back garden of number 8. The planners have much to answer for.

During his time at Lord's he did not travel very much as his work kept him on the home front, if not at Lord's, then occasionally around the grounds mostly in England. Overseas travel was for those involved with the first class game so his colleagues were frequently away for noticeable lengths of time. After his retirement he and my mother were able to break away and visit cricket playing countries abroad. For a good many years the MCC team travel arrangements for foreign tours were organised by George Wareham's company. As time passed MCC's business moved on and George evolved cricket spectating trips across the world. With Dad's contacts and knowledge he was given a free place and retained to troubleshoot when problems arose – lost tickets, failed hotel bookings, late coach arrivals, all the usual things that happen to people on holiday were left for Jim to sort out. After so many years at Lord's he knew everyone so with his mild and diplomatic demeanour there was little trouble in resolving difficulties. In fact, he and my mother had great trips staying in grand hotels, meeting many old cricket friends, officials and players, and enjoying generous, often overwhelming, hospitality at Test Match grounds in Australia, India, South Africa and the Caribbean. His helpful and courteous role at Lord's was at last rewarded. In India they were whisked away by the Maharaja of Baroda to stay in one of his palaces with the invitation 'Jim, you cannot possibly stay in that hotel'. What more could they possibly want?

My parents held their 40th wedding anniversary in the Player's Dining Room. In 1978 social occasions such as this were a rarity in the Pavilion. Gill, David and Sheila Dunbar.

EXTRAS

75 YEARS OF HOUSING

In the meantime the final twenty-six years of my working career were spent with the St Marylebone Housing Association, a local social housing charity which rented affordable flats and homes to the elderly and families on low incomes. The Association recognised that high property prices in the St John's Wood area made it almost impossible for many of those on humble MCC wages to live close by. Over the years, a number of Lord's employees, including Henry Johns and George Beeton, had homes conveniently nearby in Cochrane Street and off Abbey Road. Living five minutes walk from one's place of work saves a fair chunk of life. When you think about it – an hour there and another back, travelling five days a week for forty plus years adds up to many months, if not more, wasted in the car, bus or train. Apart from the head groundsman's flat and two others overlooking the Nursery Ground, MCC has sold all its property in Grove End Road and Elm Tree Road where the three Secretaries were once housed. In my father's day it took him all of three minutes to walk to his office.

St Marylebone Housing Association 75th Anniversary celebration at Lord's. David Dunbar, Chief Executive, with Chairman, Tony Dundas.

In 2001 over 100 dignitaries and supporters gathered in the Long Room for a reception to celebrate the Housing Association's 75th anniversary of its foundation. The Long Room is a great magnet for a prestige event and guarantees virtually a hundred per cent acceptance of invitations. So along came the Lord Mayor of Westminster and plenty of the local good and greats. Lord's has capitalised on the catering and hospitality, now in-house, and in a quality league of their own to the extent that they have generated more money out of hospitality than the gate takings from spectators. Food, drinks, service and organisation complement the venue's grand surroundings. My brief speech, as retiring Chief Executive, was, I thought, to be my swan song.

T20 FOR ALL

Over the last decade cricket watching has developed as an entertainment to meet a variety of tastes. An unusually warm evening and I jump on a 13 bus to rattle down to Lord's. Arriving at 6.15 I have missed the first ten overs, but no matter. Middlesex are doing battle with Surrey. The ground is heaving and all but full with the Pavilion jammed to the brim, so I seek an empty seat on the summit of the Tavern Stand which is a good view with the wicket on the near side, even though the seating leg-room is almost non-existent. I have never seen Lord's so well attended for a routine weekday T20 match. What a waste of electricity with the floodlights shining away on the ground still in bright sunshine.

A full Lord's buzzes with incessant chatter from the spectators. Occasionally it is interspersed with great excitement and applause for sixes or a wicket. The two sides have attracted near enough an equal balance of north and south London supporters. Most have arrived from the office and I find myself planted amongst a bunch of hooray Henries all talking money and staggering to and from their seats to fetch 4x4 carriers of plastic pint beers. The only consolation is that they import their exceedingly pretty Henriettae who bray their way through even more pints than their chaps.

The cricket is a bit peripheral but Surrey knock up a reasonably respectable total of 178 and Middlesex just about keep the lid on. Eventually their batting fails dismally thanks to several superb catches, worth the visit just for that, and finally fail to reach three figures, by which time the shadows on the pitch are foursome under the darkening skies. Chris Tremlett is bowling at a terrifying pace and Eoin Morgan nearly gets going well but holes out too soon. The home team crumple. Local residents complain about 'light pollution' and traffic but if you buy a home adjacent to a major sporting venue what do you expect – anyway it's not often and the inconvenience, if any, could not be more benign. The cheerful crowds melt away quickly as I wander back to the bus stop – I enjoyed that. Some people I know are highly scornful of limited over games but why not savour all cricket, learn and appreciate the different versions.

OLYMPIC LEGEND

The London 2012 Olympics did not feature cricket, nor for that matter, rugby (of any sort), golf, squash, croquet or fives. So one must banish disingenuous thoughts that the rest of the world is reluctant to be reminded of no more than a sample of Britain's or, more precisely, England's sporting legacies. Indeed, in the nineteenth century MCC formalised the rules of tennis as well as cricket. At least we tried for Monsieur Pierre de Coubertin with French cricket! No matter. The International Olympic Committee was gracious enough to accept Lord's as the venue for the archers, who came not from Ambridge, but all over the world to shoot their arrows. I dread to think how many MCC committee man hours were exhausted on taking the decision of handing over the ground for several weeks at the height of the cricket season. Let alone what happens if a stray projectile or two fizzes into where a good length ball should pitch. It was a brave and good commitment.

MCC offered placatory tickets to members so, having had no luck with my Olympic stadium application, I duly put in for and got four tickets for a day in an early round of archery. The success of the Olympics has rapidly moved into the legend of our lifetimes and I am glad to say Lord's played its part superbly, albeit on a relatively modest scale. Two purple cloth-clad (the Olympic livery) stands for five thousand spectators were erected, forming a corridor between the Pavilion and the square, with the toxopholites shooting across the square towards the Media Centre.

The whole event was thoroughly un-Lord's-like from start to finish. Raucous rock music was interspersed with a very jolly commentary explaining to the enthusiastic, but largely ignorant, crowd what was going on. Dress code was refreshingly optional, in fact non-existent. A bunch of young chaps dressed as Robin Hoods or his Merry Men (plus a Maid Marian or two) and people from all corners of the planet had gathered to watch. Union jacks and flags from many nations were waving everywhere in the bright sun. There was not an MCC steward in sight and the cheerful volunteers in charge were unconcerned about the uninhibited and at times exuberant crowd behaviour, not to mention the lack of jackets and ties in and around the Pavilion.

For those members of the public who wanted a go, the Coronation Garden was set up as a short archery range. Very low-tech bows and arrows were hired out to long queues. W G Grace remained resolutely forward defensive as arrows whistled past his statue and sometimes hit the targets.

The real archers took it all very seriously and everyone fell silent when an arrow was to be loosed off – the idea being to hit the centre of the target, about the size and colour of a grapefruit, for ten points, and less for the outer rings. Considering the distance of some seventy metres and the vagaries of wind, it was remarkable that nines and tens were commonplace and anything less than an eight points was greeted with a sympathetic moan from the crowd. It was pleasing that competitors from all countries were generously applauded for

Olympic flags flown from the Pavilion.

A new configuration of stands for watching The London 2012 Olympics from the Pavilion.

their obvious skills. The only Brit that morning was quickly eliminated but got rapturous cheers before he triumphantly scuttled off, not to be seen again until Rio. Everyone was involved, and having great fun.

I am reminded of a photograph of the South African team being presented to the King in 1935 in front of the Pavilion. The outfield shows a disconcerting surface of patchy, lumpy, bumpy grass. This fielder's nightmare was a far cry from the immaculately smooth, green and manicured surfaces of the twenty-first century. Nowadays, the test of a fielder's dream outfield is a well-driven ball heading towards the boundary without a bobble or deviation on its journey.

Ten days after the archery there's a Test Match against South Africa scheduled, so what of the pitch and outfield? The stands and Olympic paraphernalia have vanished, a third of the outfield grass has been re-laid and the ground appears near perfect with hardly a mark or undulation to be seen. Sadly such a remarkable feat of planning and groundsmanship, not to mention the generous inducement from the Olympic authorities, aka us taxpayers, were all in vain. The England cricketers were unable to reward Lord's, being well thrashed by South Africa as though nothing strange had ever happened. Nevertheless, a gold medal and congratulations must go to all at Lord's for an unusual and thoroughly entertaining venture.

WEDDING BELL

Our final Lord's chapter started with the ringing of the St John's Wood Church bell (being a former chapel of ease, there's only one) for the wedding of Lucy, our beautiful daughter. By the roundabout, it is a mere cricket ball's throw from Lord's and the cupola is visible from the higher vantage points in the ground. My wife and I were married there in 1979, Lucy was christened there and both my parents' memorial services were held at St John's – a place of both joyful and sad memories for the Dunbar family.

In the middle of the roundabout is the fine statue of St George slaying the dragon – as Lucy chose to marry her George I am still trying to work out the symbolism, if any, of this coincidence! We had found an early August Saturday in 2010 when no Lord's cricket was scheduled so the Pavilion was booked for the reception. Some while later I was told that an important international benefit match of some sort had been proposed for that day but MCC clearly did not relish renegotiating the date with Lucy. There is no doubt who would have won!

So on the happy day our 113 lucky guests straggled from the church along St John's Wood Road, through the Grace Gates, and up to the Pavilion roof terrace for their champers and canapés (as Lord's insists on calling nibbles). If a reception needs a view then the renovated roof terrace is the place. The sun shone, as did the whole stadium, the grass so immaculate but, oh dear, what, no cricket? Intriguingly a number of the drinkers sat gazing across the ground each deeply engrossed in their own fantasy game being played out far below – although I was uncertain what my cousin's young children from Germany were thinking! The electronic scoreboard offered endless scope for awful messages like 'Lucy and George – a Great Match', 'Congratulations, W G Grace' and so they went on.

Soon we descended to the Long Room which was all laid up for the wedding meal. I had been somewhat apprehensive about an edict issued in the MCC

Lucy Robson, nee Dunbar, and husband George make their way down the aisle.

Father of the bride delivers his wedding speech in the Long Room.

The scoreboard messages!

contract that the members' formal dress code must be observed by all guests in the Pavilion. Knowing that some of Lucy and George's friends did not own jackets, let alone ties, I had obtained a slightly begrudging email from the Chief Executive's office waiving the rule. As a precaution, I had a copy in my pocket in case the message had failed to permeate from on high to the stewards. In fact I need not have worried, the stewards were a delight, performing all sorts of unlikely services including pushing buggies with babies into the lift. They have transformed from the grumpy old days and now exude pleasant courtesy and helpfulness. Unexpectedly, several of George's friends turned out to be keen cricketers but had never been to Lord's – they were given an impromptu tour of the England dressing room between the starter and main course which made their day. This was my second Long Room speech, made some sixty years after I first entered the great temple of cricket.

As I said, it had always been a dream of mine – passing through the Long Room to descend the steps to play on the ground – but that never happened. On the other hand, as father of the bride, did I ever imagine that a greater pleasure would be wishing my daughter and her husband unending health and happiness together. Her grandfather and grandmother would have been happy and proud too. I wonder if their great grandson, now aged three, and his younger brother, will one day play at Lord's.

STUMPS

Lord's in 1950s and onwards

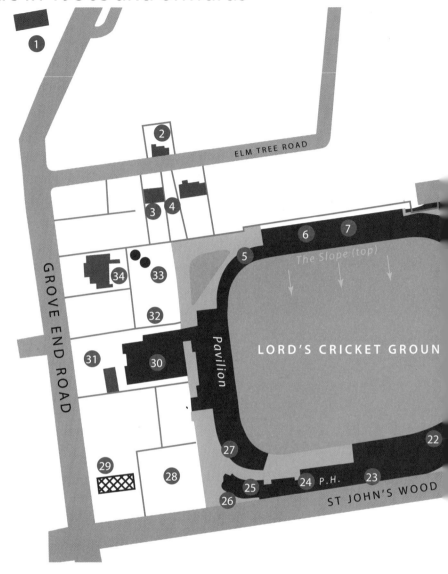

KEY

1. EMI Recording Studios
2. Old farm cottage and buildings
3. Our home – 6 Elm Tree Road
4. Lord's Drive and Net
5. A Stand (now Warner Stand)
6. Grand Stand
7. Father Time
8. Beatle House
9. North Gate
10. Arbours
11. St John's Wood Burial Ground
12. Memorial Tulip Tree to Brian Johnston
13. St John's Wood Church
14. Statue of St John the Baptist
15. Statue of St George and the Dragon
16. Warsop's Bat factory
17. Power station chimney
18. Arbours
19. Head groundsman Lodge
20. Free Seats
21. East Gate
22. Mound Stand
23. Main Gate
24. Lord's Tavern
25. Clock Tower and
26. Grace Gates
27. Q Stand